Research Methods
for Community Health and Welfare

Research Methods for Community Health and Welfare

an Introduction

KARL E. BAUMAN
Department of Maternal and Child Health
School of Public Health
The University of North Carolina at Chapel Hill

New York Oxford
Oxford University Press
1980

Library of Congress Cataloging in Publication Data

Bauman, Karl E.
 Research methods for community health and welfare.

 Bibliography: p.
 Includes index.
 1. Public heath—Research. 2. Public welfare—
Research. 3. Research I Title.
[DNLM: 1. Community health services. 2. Research
design. 3. Social welfare. WA546.1 B347r]
RA440.85.B38   362.1'07'2   80-11934
ISBN 0-19-502698-5
ISBN 0-19-502699-3 pbk.

Foreword

For the modern student who is concerned with the planning, administration, evaluation, and formation of policy for health, welfare, or educational services, knowledge of research methods is an essential, not a luxury, Too often our ineffective services are due to an uncritical reading of the published research or to our failure to do even the most simple kind of research to aid the planning or evaluating of our programs. Policy decisions are seldom based on adequate research, and often on none at all. The literature in all of the human services is filled with both good and bad research; and unless one can distinguish the two, totally unjustified conclusions may be drawn.

This in no way implies that the average student of human services, whether in a bachelor's or master's degree program (or dedicated to self-study), needs to become an expert in every phase of human services research. It does mean that he or she must have sufficient knowledge to be, above all things, a discriminating reader of the literature relevant to his or her interests. Moreover, in all probability, the student will have to do some research to plan or evaluate programs, because this is increasingly being required for initial or continued funding. The student may never actually do much research, but he or she will almost certainly have to work with research people in the course of a career.

During almost a decade of teaching an introductory research methods course to master's level public health students, as well as some medical students, my greatest obstacle and source of dissatisfaction was the lack of an adequate textbook. The half-dozen or so that I tried have failed for a number of reasons, including being: wordy, unclear, too clinically oriented, too sketchy, too detailed, or too specialized. The only one which was fairly satisfactory went out of print! This forced me, in part, to build the course on existing examples of research in the literature, which was a major improvement. However, the students continued to need and want a textbook, and a colleague and I had almost decided that we would have to write the text ourselves. Fortunately, Dr. Bauman's book came to my attention through Oxford University Press, when I was asked to review an earlier version. It was immediately apparent that Dr. Bauman's draft had the potential for being the textbook I was seeking. In the fall of 1978, I was able to use a draft of his text with my class for the first time, as a field trial, and the results were gratifying. The text provided a conceptual base that freed up class time for clarification rather than routine presentation of the basics. The terminology was standard, the examples were well chosen and quite relevant to our concerns, the writing was lucid, the length was right, and most important, the students like the book! They found it helpful rather than, as so often in the past, confusing.

Another important advantage is that Dr. Bauman uses two published studies, one of health services and one of social services, as a common thread running through several chapters, to illustrate his principles. This is helpful in demonstrating the relevance and interrelatedness of the research topics, especially if the students have copies of these published studies to read from the beginning of the course. As they reread the studies in light of the text, what may have been confusing to them becomes clear. Not only do the students come to understand *what* was done, but more important, *why* it was done and what compromises were necessary in the real world. Thus, the textbook and the real-life research reinforce each other as the class progresses. I had previously found both the study of actual research and the use of a textbook essential for such a class; for the first time, the two were intimately related and thus mutually reinforcing.

Dr. Bauman's textbook is only moderately detailed, because it seeks primarily to communicate an understanding of the basic logic and methods of research. This makes it generally useful to research courses in many different fields of human services. It has enough detail to communicate the research principles common to all fields, but it is not filled with details only relevant to one specialty or another. I have found the text easy to supplement with the study of actual research reports, with more detailed readings on special topics, and with practical exercises, such as writing research protocols.

The clarity of approach and organization of this text is sufficient to make it useful for self-study by those practitioners who want to understand research but do not have the time to take formal course work.

I hope this textbook will make an important contribution to the improvement of human services; I believe it will.

James F. Jekel, M.D., M.P.H.
Associate Professor of Public Health

Yale Medical School
New Haven
June 4, 1979

Acknowledgments

If my hopes for this book are realized, they will have been greatly assisted by insight and encouragement from others. Valuable comments on one or several chapters were provided by Dan Freeman, Gary G. Koch, Carl Henley, and Sherman James. James Jekel, J. Richard Udry, and Elizabeth Bryan criticized two versions of the manuscript, and to each of them I express double thanks for their substantial contributions. This book also benefits from constructive criticisms by James Jekel's students at Yale and many of my own students at the University of North Carolina at Chapel Hill. The editorial and substantive talents of Jeffrey W. House are reflected throughout the book.

I would have never written this book in the absence of invariable support from my parents, Dr. and Mrs. E.K. Bauman. I will always be deeply grateful to them for this, as for so much else. And as many authors have said at this place in their books, my wife and children did sacrifice while the book was being prepared. To the credit of Judy, Jenny, Jay, and Katy, however, I suspect that on balance they were happier because they shared my belief that the product could contribute to others. The book would have remained forthcoming without the positive environment they provided.

K.E.B.

Contents

1. Introduction,   3

2. The Hypothesis and Theory   7
   Definition of a Hypothesis   7
   Functions of Hypotheses   8
   Criteria for Adequate Hypotheses   10
   Theory   11
   Conclusion   15

3. Causal Research   16
   Independent and Dependent Variables   17
   Evidence for Inferring Causality   18
   Other Variables   21

4. Intervention Designs   23
   Examples and Symbols   23
   One Group-After Only   25
   Two Group- After Only   27
   One Group-Before After   30
   Two Group-Before After   35
   A Note on Matching   39
   An Introduction to Random Allocation   40

Two Group-After Only with Random Allocation   43
Two Group-Before After with Random Allocation   44
Four Group-Two Before and Four After
    with Random Allocation   45
Several Other Considerations   46
A Comment on Evaluation   48

5. Nonintervention Designs   50
Cross-Sectional Design   51
Trend Design   55
Panel Design   56
Additional Thoughts on Nonintervention Designs   60

6. Descriptive Research   63
The Purpose of Descriptive Research and Selected
    Examples   64
On the Importance of Descriptive Research   65
Comparison of Descriptive and Causal Research   65
On Causal Inferences from Descriptive Research   66

7. Samples and Populations   68
An Introduction to Probability Sampling   69
Types of Probability Samples   72
Nonprobability Samples   73
Types of Nonprobability Samples   74
Selection Bias   75
Attrition   76
Sample Size   77
The Sampling Fraction   80
Sampling and Other Ingredients of Research   80

8. Measurement   83
The Myth That "Some Variables Can't Be Measured"   84
Measurement Error and Its Sources   85
Reliability   88
Validity   92
On Validity and Reliability   97
Multiple-Item Scales   97
On the Fineness of Measures   100

Data Collection Methods   100
More Detailed Sources   101

9. Contingency Table Analysis   103
The Two-Variable Table   103
Analyses with More Than Two Variables   105
Intervening Variables   109
An Example from an Actual Study   110
Other Considerations   112
Limitations of Contingency Table Analysis   114
Other Methods of Controlling for Spurious Association   116

10. Statistical Significance and Strength   119
Levels of Significance   119
Two-Variate Tests and Level of Measurement   122
Statistical Significance and Contingency Table
    Analysis   124
Multivariate Tests   127
Sample Size and Fraction   131
Strength of Association   133
Statistical and Practical Significance   134
Statistical Significance in Descriptive Research   137
Tests of Statistical Significance and Probability
    Samples   138
Other Considerations   139

Epilogue   141

Index   143

Research Methods
for Community Health and Welfare

1
Introduction

Many important issues are encountered by those who attempt to improve the health and welfare of communities. The following questions come to mind:

1. Will reducing the caseload of social workers from sixty to twenty-five families facilitate family functioning?
2. Could replacement-level fertility have been approached in the United States in the 1970s if all unwanted births to the poor had been prevented?
3. Does comprehensive and family-focused pediatric care reduce morbidity more than services that are relatively episodic, fragmented, and impersonal?
4. Will an intensive education program by nurses for the chronically ill increase compliance with the plans prescribed for the patients by physicians?

It would seem that reducing the caseload of social workers from sixty to twenty-five families must contribute positively to family functioning. I have often seen how little time can be devoted to counseling when the caseload is heavy and often observed what good results follow when the social worker has the time to provide in-depth counsel. Many social workers agree with me. Some eminent demographers believed that replacement-level fertility—the number of births required for zero population growth—could have been approached in the United States in the 1970s if the poor had no unwanted births. Moreover, the poor were especially likely to have unwanted babies, and it was to this group that the federal birth control program was directed. So one might conclude that if the poor had had no unwanted births, United States fertility in the 1970s would have been reduced substantially and perhaps brought to the replacement level. Similarly, comprehensive pediatric care must have a significant impact on morbidity. Many health professionals assert this, and there has been an enormous investment of time and money in this beneficial form of care. An intensive program of education by nurses should result in more chronically ill patients following their doctors' orders. Careful instruction about using medicine and following other prescriptions must be prerequisite to the knowledge and motivation that lead to positive health-related behavior.

The beliefs expressed above are derived mainly from common sense, experience, intuition, tradition, and authority. Researchers address these questions quite differently. Wallace (1967) selected families in need of social service, assigned social workers to caseloads of sixty or twenty-five families, and for two years systematically documented and compared trends on many different dimensions of family functioning. I applied simple mathematics to data that had been carefully collected by others to estimate what fertility would have been in the early 1970s if the poor had had no unwanted births (Bauman, 1972). Alpert and his colleagues (1976) observed morbidity over time in families which were comparable except that some had received an intensive comprehensive medical care program and others had not. Tagliacozzo and associates (1974) introduced an innovative education program to some patients while giving the usual program to other patients, and then compared these groups on several measures of compliance.

If research always yielded the same conclusions as the other sources of knowledge, then I would not use it because of the time and money involved. Moreover, the other sources can be correct, and research does not always produce conclusions which are true. However, research and the other sources for establishing facts and principles often yield inconsistent conclusions. All the studies mentioned above produced findings which ran counter to the expectations of many experienced professionals: The reduction in caseload did not enhance family functioning; family planning for the poor could not account for replacement-level fertility in the United States; comprehensive medical care did not decrease morbidity; and the educational program for the chronically ill did not increase compliance.

Research, when conducted properly, is the best method for establishing facts and principles, and community health and welfare are more likely to be improved when decisions are based on fact rather than plausible fiction. Since the studies cited above used sound research methods, I am willing to accept their conclusions and reject beliefs not based on research. All professionals should have some understanding of research methods in order to be able to sift facts from erroneous beliefs in their field.

This book is an introduction for those who plan to do research in community health and welfare or for researchers at the edge of the field. It is written mainly for students who will become service providers, policy makers, program administrators, and consultants. There are three main reasons why nonresearchers need a basic understanding of research methods. First, like most other things, research varies in quality and can be interpreted incorrectly. It is essential that the methods and their relative merits be understood before the results are used to make decisions. In making decisions, one should weigh various studies in accordance with how well the research was done. Second, an acquaintance with research methods is necessary for effective communication. This need is often made clear when a researcher is used as a consultant or a researcher and a nonresearcher are collaborating on a study. The researcher may want to use procedures that strike the nonresearcher as unduly time-consuming or unnecessary. Or, without help from other practitioners, the researcher may be unable to formulate precisely a research question or to interpret readily the findings of a study. They need mutual guidance, which requires some common understanding of the methods used. Third, persons unfamiliar with the research process sometimes do not use its results in their decision making because the methods are incompletely understood. Thus, research may be treated as irrelevant to the important decisions at hand.

This book introduces many research techniques. Chapter 2 deals with hypotheses and theory. For research to be conducted successfully, well-formulated hypotheses which can be accepted or rejected are essential and preferably should be rooted in a more general theoretical framework. Chapter 3 introduces basic features of causal inference and the types of evidence needed for making inferences about causality. Policies and programs, and studies which pertain to them, are focused primarily upon causal inferences. Chapters 4 and 5 describe and assess different research designs which are commonly used to test causal hypotheses. Chapter 6 considers descriptive research. The findings of descriptive studies are extremely important for use in decision making even though they do not contribute directly to causal inferences. Chapter 7 contains a discussion of the use of population samples to test causal and descriptive hypotheses which pertain to populations. Chapter 8 deals with measurement; all research depends upon acceptably accurate measurement. Chapters 9 and 10 describe two of the most common approaches for analyzing data: contingency table analysis and statistical significance and strength. Several concluding remarks are offered in the Epilogue.

References

Alpert, Joel J.; Robertson, Leon S.; Kosa, John; Heagarty, Margaret C.; and Haggerty, Robert J. (1976) "Delivery of Health Care for Children: Report of an Experiment." *Pediatrics* 57:917–30.

Bauman, Karl E. (1972) "The Poor as a 'Perfect Contraceptive Population' and Zero Population Growth." *Demography* 9:507–10.

Tagliacozzo, Daisy M.; Luskin, Diana Biordi; Lashof, Joyce C.; and Ima, Kenji (1974) "Nurse Intervention and Patient Behavior: An Experimental Study." *American Journal of Public Health* 64:596–603.

Wallace, David (1967) "The Chemung County Evaluation of Casework Service to Dependent Multiproblem Families: Another Problem Outcome." *Social Service Review* 41:379–89.

2
The Hypothesis and Theory

Definition of a hypothesis

A *hypothesis* is a proposition that is to be, and can be, tested by research. Hypotheses are tentative rather than definitive statements, and they must have the potential of being accepted or rejected by research. Here are a few examples:

1. Among women who receive prenatal care in a clinic, those who have early and extended contact with their infants in the hospital are more likely to be attached to their infants than those who do not.
2. Persons who smoke cigarettes are more likely to die from lung cancer than those who do not.
3. Most patients who receive organized family planning services also receive other public assistance.
4. The percentage of children aged one to four immunized for polio increased between 1965 and 1975 in the United States.

It should be emphasized that a hypothesis must have the capacity to be judged true or false by research. Many statements do not have this capacity and thus are not hypotheses. Consider, for example, the following:

1. Cigarette smoking should be a felony.
2. Women are superior to men.

The proposition that cigarette smoking should be a felony is a value judgment, and value judgments per se cannot be judged by research to be true or false. So this proposition is not a hypothesis. Many different hypotheses, however, do have a bearing on the value judgment that cigarette smoking should be a felony—for example, "cigarette smokers die younger than persons who don't smoke," "women who smoke during pregnancy are more likely to have low birth weight infants than those who do not," and "most people in the United States believe that cigarette smoking should be a felony"—but the value judgment itself cannot be accepted or rejected by research.

There are no acceptable methods for judging some propositions. Although some people have stated that women are superior to men, this cannot be regarded as a hypothesis because the meaning of "superior" here is nonspecific and thus unclear. As a result, we could not classify people according to their level of superiority, and that classification is prerequisite for testing the proposition through research. We could apply research to accept or reject such hypotheses as "women live longer than men," "women have fewer chronic illnesses than men," and "women have higher IQs than men." However, we cannot at present do research to test the idea that women are superior to men; it would be impossible to reach a consensus on the meaning of superiority in this context.

Hypotheses are not unequivocally determined by research to be true or false. Conclusions regarding research hypotheses are probabilities rather than absolute certainties. Research is not free of error. This equivocal feature of research will be discussed throughout this book.

Functions of hypotheses

A major function of hypotheses is to guide research. More specifically, adequately developed hypotheses contribute substantially to such activities as identifying the types of data to be collected, determining what cases should be included for study, designing and implementing the research plan, organizing data in patterns that can be interpreted, and drawing conclusions from the research.

This guidance function of hypotheses is especially apparent when data are collected without hypotheses. Although painful to consider, such research efforts do occur in health and welfare agencies; some have gathered data for years only because the information would some day be needed to determine if the agency goals have been achieved. These data remain unanalyzed, or if they are examined, the conclusions are often methodologically indefensible or cannot be translated for use in relevant decisions about goal achievement. Why is this effort so unproductive? Frequently it is because there were no hypotheses to guide the research. The notion of determining whether agency goals have been achieved is usually too poorly defined to be judged true or false by research and therefore is not a hypothesis. The statement is not useful in determining what data should be gathered, how the research plan should be designed, or how the data might be manipulated to address important questions.

Now imagine an agency that perceived the same need to determine if agency goals have been achieved but took another step and identified the goals as: 1. decreasing economic dependency, 2. decreasing inappropriate institutionalization of children, and 3. reducing abuse and neglect. On the basis of these goals and an understanding of research methods, the agency could then formulate three hypotheses: Persons who receive services from the agency, when compared with those who do not, are 1. more likely to become economically independent, 2. less likely to have inappropriately institutionalized children, and 3. less likely to have family members who have been abused and neglected. From these propositions, we know that information must be gathered from persons who receive services from the agency as well as those who do not. We also know that the agency must be able to identify the persons who become economically independent, have children inappropriately institutionalized, and have family members who are abused and neglected. When analyzing the data, we know that the persons who received services must be compared with those who did not.

Those who use the research of others for making decisions about programs and policy also depend on adequate research hypotheses. Most basically, hypotheses contribute to the existence of the research used. Persons must compare the hypotheses with their own questions to see if the research is relevant to their needs. Research utilizers must also compare the hypotheses with the research methods used in order to assess the quality of the research before determining how the results can contribute to their work. Collaboration between the researcher and others requires a clear and mutual understanding of what the research is about, and in this regard there is no worthy substitute for adequately formulated hypotheses.

Criteria for adequate hypotheses

Hypotheses vary with respect to how effectively they guide research. Among the most important features of adequate hypotheses are clarity and specificity. If there is consensus about what a hypothesis means, it is usually sufficiently clear and specific for guiding research. If there is difficulty understanding exactly what the hypothesis means, or what research methods might be used to test it, then the hypothesis is too vague and general.

Consider again the hypothesis that persons who receive services from an agency, compared with those who do not, are more likely to become economically independent. There could be disagreement on what is meant by "receive services" and "economically independent." One person might believe that a client has received services if one hour of consultation has been given; another might believe that more extensive involvement is needed; and still another might believe that some form of economic subsidy is necessary. Does "economically independent" mean that the client is receiving no funds from the agency, or receiving no public funds at all, or relying on no one for economic sufficiency?

Definitions of the two concepts embodied in the hypothesis

could make it clearer and more specific, and hence provide more explicit guidance for research. Suppose they were defined as follows:

receive services: to receive direct payment of money from the agency for one or more months.

economically independent: to receive no direct payment of money from any public agency for one year.

This clarifies matters considerably. Now we know, for instance, that we are to study clients who received direct payment of money from the agency for one or more months, and that a subject who receives direct payment from public funds administered by another agency will be classified as economically dependent.

Theory

A *theory* consists of one or more general and logically interrelated propositions offered to explain a class of phenomena. Theories have functions which are so basic to research that theory, research, and hypotheses tend to be interdependent.

We will return to the definition of theory after considering as an example the health belief theory, which has obvious implications for a wide range of activities related to the health and welfare of communities. Summaries of this theory and extensive citations to the pertinent research literature are given by Rosenstock (1966) and Becker and Maiman (1975).

The health belief theory attempts to explain why some people behave in ways that lead to good health. A sketch of the theory is given in Figure 2.1. Box B of the diagram requires explanation. The theory postulates that there are four immediate determinants of health-related behavior: 1. "susceptibility," the degree to which poor health is anticipated; 2. "seriousness," the degree of severity perceived to be associated with poor health; 3. "benefits/costs," the ratio of positive to negative results of a health-related behavior; and 4. "cue to action," a stimulus for triggering health-related behavior.

Figure 2.1. Health Belief Theory

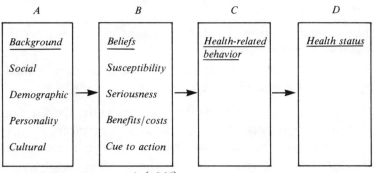

Adapted from Rosenstock (1966).

There are many propositions related to this theory. One is that people who believe they are susceptible to poor health are more likely to act in ways that avoid this problem than people who do not see themselves as susceptible. Another proposition is that people who rate high in all four areas—susceptibility, seriousness, benefits/costs, and cues to action—are more likely to act in ways that promote good health than people who do not. Other variables are also included in the theory. As box A suggests, social, demographic, personal, and cultural factors are viewed as influencing the beliefs which in turn influence behavior. Thus, another proposition of the theory is that persons with different backgrounds receive a cue to action in varying degrees.

From this incomplete discussion, one can see that the health belief theory consists of general and logically interrelated propositions which aim to explain a class of phenomena. The propositions are stated very generally, without reference to specific background factors, beliefs, behaviors, or health status. Indeed, the theory purports to account for any behavior related to health. Among the many behaviors covered by the theory are obtaining immunization, smoking cigarettes, complying with medical regimens, and participating in any type of screening program. The broad range of background variables is also stated in general terms, unrelated to health beliefs or practices. The theory is not restricted to any subgroup of people. Research has addressed some of the theory's propositions, at least indirectly, as indicated by many citations in Rosenstock (1966) and Becker and Maiman (1975).

The health belief theory can be used to compare the meanings of the words "hypothesis" and "theory." The full theory could never be tested directly by research because it is much too general. As the earlier discussion of hypotheses indicates, statements must be quite specific before they can provide the guidance necessary for implementing research. We would need to know the specific health consequences, health-related behaviors, beliefs, and background factors to be considered before proceeding very far with research. Another feature of theories that precludes testing this one directly, and completely, is that all background, belief, behavior, and health variables would have to be included in order to accept or reject the whole theory. I cannot envision a study, or group of studies, that would encompass all these variables.

It is easy to see, however, that a direct derivative of the theory could be examined by research. Although any health-related behavior could serve as an example, consider the decision of parents to have their child immunized. According to the theory, a child is likely to be immunized against measles if the parent 1. believes that measles might occur in the absence of immunization (susceptibility), 2. believes that measles would have extremely unpleasant consequences for the child or family (seriousness), 3. believes that such benefits as positive health and well-being outweigh such costs as the bus fare required to get to a clinic and the amount of time that would be spent waiting there (benefits/costs), and 4. learns that experts are predicting an epidemic of measles (cue to action). If one or more of these beliefs is not held by the parent, the child is less likely to be immunized. We might hypothesize that persons without a high school education would be less likely than persons with a high school education to have their child immunized; the former consider their child less susceptible to measles, the consequences of measles less serious, the costs to outweigh the benefits, and they are less exposed to cues for action. This derivative of the theory is much more specific than the theory itself, and therefore is more amenable to testing through research.

Hypotheses are specific and, by definition, can be tested by research and can guide research. Theories are, by definition, too general to be examined directly in their entirety by research. However, they contain principles which can be translated into hypotheses that can be examined by research. One way to view the relationship between hypotheses and theory is that hypotheses serve as the link between theory and research: Research is conducted to test hypotheses which are suggested by theory, and tested hypotheses become embodied as principles in an improved theory.

Theories have important functions, some of which are:

1. To *summarize knowledge* about a class of phenomena. An accurate summary of knowledge is of such obvious value that it requires no further discussion.
2. To *integrate knowledge.* The hundreds of studies cited by Rosenstock (1966) and Becker and Maiman (1975) provide an example of how seemingly isolated studies can gain significance when they are integrated by a theory.
3. To *generate hypotheses* which, when tested, add to knowledge. An untested link in a theory is ripe for formulation of hypotheses to be tested by research, and the integration provided by a theory makes it easier to identify an untested link. Studying the health belief theory might lead to the identification of an untested health-related behavior, which could stimulate hypotheses to be examined by research. Tested hypotheses, in turn, contribute to the refinement of theory.
4. To guide *hypothesis formulation.* If one were studying the influence of perceived seriousness of lung cancer on smoking behavior, the health belief model could stimulate hypotheses incorporating susceptibility, benefits/costs, cues to action, and background factors. Without the theory, such hypotheses probably would not be advanced.

5. To *restrict the field* and thus make research more manageable. If we attempted to enumerate the possible factors in lung cancer, we would probably identify many more than could be studied. A theory would narrow our focus and thereby make the research possibilities more realistic.

6. To help make *decisions about hypotheses* that are tested by research. An accepted hypothesis related to a theory firmly grounded in other research gains credibility over an accepted hypothesis that has no basis in theory.

7. To *stimulate productive research.* Research based solely on speculation contributes less to our knowledge than research guided, at least in part, by the facts and principles derived from earlier research and embodied by theory.

8. To assist *decision making on policies and programs.* Health and welfare professionals cannot always wait for research findings to make their decisions, and their specific problem may never have been studied.

Conclusion

The centrality of hypotheses in research cannot be overemphasized. They must exist before research can begin, and they permeate all aspects of a successful study. Hypotheses and theories are interdependent and essential in the expansion of knowledge. Kerlinger (1973) and Lastrucci (1963) can be recommended for their introductory discussions of hypotheses and theory.

References

Becker, M. H.; and Maiman, L. A. (1975) "Sociobehavioral Determinants of Compliance with Health and Medical Recommendations." *Medical Care* 13:10–24.

Kerlinger, Fred N. (1973) *Foundations of Behavioral Research.* 2nd. ed. New York: Holt, Rinehart and Winston. Pp. 16–27

Lastrucci, Carlo L. (1963) *The Scientific Approach.* Cambridge, Mass.: Shenkman. Pp. 52–119.

Rosenstock, I. W. (1966) "Why People Use Health Services." *Milbank Memorial Fund Quarterly* 44:94–124.

3

Causal Research

Causation occurs when something produces or forces something else (Blalock, 1964). Most community health and welfare activities attempt to *cause* things to happen. And those who act often think and behave in terms of causation. They think, for instance, that maternity and infant care programs will reduce prematurity and perinatal death, that family planning will reduce the birth rate, that methadone will help alleviate the problem of heroin addiction, that immunization will prevent smallpox, and so on.

Causation is obviously basic to many of the assumptions which underlie programs and policies. Two examples should suffice. It has been inferred that smoking is detrimental to health. That assumption is basic to such federal policies and programs as the ban on television advertising of cigarettes, the health warning on cigarette packages, and numerous mass media programs with anti-smoking content. A major assumption that guides family planning policy and programs in the United States is that low income leads to contraceptive behavior that results in unwanted pregnancies. Thus, education and contraceptive services are provided for the poor, and it is assumed that their contraceptive behavior will change; in this way, the goal of the policy and programs—to reduce unwanted fertility in the United States—will be achieved.

Table 3.1. Selected causal inferences with variables in italics and values indicated

Caseload of social worker
  a. 25 families
  b. 60 families   ⟶
	Family functioning
	  a. Good
	  b. Poor

Expertise of physician and nurse
  a. Applied
  b. Not applied   ⟶
	Health of patient
	  a. Good
	  b. Poor

Maternity and infant care
  a. Received
  b. Not received   ⟶
	Perinatal mortality
	  a. Low
	  b. High

Smoke
  a. Yes
  b. No   ⟶
	Health
	  a. Bad
	  b. Good

State of battery
  a. Not defective
  b. Defective   ⟶
	State of auto engine
	  a. Operating
	  b. Not operating

If the improvement of community health and welfare depends on the validity of such causal reasoning, then it is important to test the reasoning by translating it into hypotheses for research. Research is often conducted to test hypotheses that are framed in terms of such causal linkages.

Independent and dependent variables

Several definitions here will save many words on later pages. Table 3.1 summarizes some earlier examples of causal reasoning. The arrow represents causation.

A *variable* is anything that varies, that is, has different values. Many variables have crossed our path already, and the words in italics in Table 3.1 are variables. Listed under each variable are two different values it might have.

An *independent variable* is thought to be the cause of, or influence upon, another variable(s). All variables to the left of the arrow in Table 3.1 are considered independent because we presume that they determine the other variable. A *dependent variable* is thought to be caused or affected by another variable(s). All variables to the right of the arrow in Table 3.1 are dependent variables because we consider them to be determined or influenced by the other variable.

Only two values were assigned to each variable in Table 3.1, but many more could have been included. This is true of many variables, and the number of values researchers give them often depends on practical limitations of carrying out the research as well as the inherent nature of the variables.

Evidence for inferring causality

We are reasonably secure in inferring that one variable (dependent) was caused by another (independent) when research shows that:

1. There is an association between the independent and dependent variables,
2. The dependent variable varied after occurrence of the independent variable, and
3. The association between the independent and dependent variables is probably not spurious.

To have evidence that an association or relationship exists between independent and dependent variables is to show that their values vary with one another, that a change in the value of one variable is accompanied by a change in the value of the other variable. If the probability of health impairment is .05 among smokers and .01 for nonsmokers, then there is evidence of an association between smoking and health impairment because a change in one is accompanied by a change in the other. If the probability of impaired health is .03 for both smokers and nonsmokers, then there would be evidence of no association between the variables, and from this we would probably infer that smoking does not cause impaired health.

A causal inference usually cannot be supported by evidence of association alone; among other things, it is necessary to know if the dependent variable varied after the independent variable. One variable cannot be produced by another unless it occurs after the other. Evidence that people began smoking and later injured their health would support the inference that smoking causes impaired health. If people injured their health and then began smoking, however, the assumption that impaired health resulted from smoking would be untenable.

An association between presumably independent and dependent variables is *spurious* when it results from something other than a causal link between the two variables. We might have evidence that smokers are more likely than nonsmokers to have impaired health, as well as evidence that smoking began first. However, the association might not be causal. Suppose that old people are more likely to smoke than young people, and old people are more likely to have impaired health as a result of their age but not smoking. Thus, the association between smoking and impaired health could be spurious rather than causal. The more variables we are able to rule out as possibly producing a spurious association between the supposedly independent and dependent variables, the more assured we are when inferring causality.

Evidence of association alone is usually insufficient for inferring causation. Sales of suntan lotion and the number of drownings are probably associated. However, we cannot conclude from this association that suntan lotion produces or forces drowning, or that drowning causes an increase in the sale of suntan lotion. The likelihood of forest fires increases with the number of forest rangers, but we cannot infer that this is a causal association. Many variables vary after other variables with substantial regularity, but we often cannot presume that these represent causal connections. We cannot conclude, for example, that childhood produces or forces adulthood because adulthood always occurs after childhood, or that night and day are causally related because one can considered to invariably follow the other. We can associate variables we consider independent and dependent and show that the dependent variable varied after the independent variable, but there is always the chance that some other variable—perhaps one that is unknown to the researcher—is actually producing or forcing the dependent variable. We might, through techniques described later in this book, conclude that age accounts for the relationship between smoking and health impairment. Does that mean that age is a cause of health impairment, and that the relationship between smoking and health impairment is spurious? Maybe it does, but we cannot be certain. Perhaps another variable associated with age— such as use of health services, or some unknown variable—rather than age is actually producing or forcing health impairment. Since our variables and their linkages do not operate in a vacuum, immune from the possible influence of many other variables, there is always some chance that what we think is cause and effect really is not.

Researchers are sometimes criticized by nonresearchers for reporting the findings of their causal research with a qualified phrase such as "the evidence tends to suggest that there might be a causal relationship between. . ." rather than declaring cause and effect unequivocally. This criticism is improper. Causality can never be proved beyond a shadow of a doubt through research or any other procedure, and therefore conclusions about causality should always be qualified.

Why can causality never be concluded without qualification? As Blalock (1964) and others have indicated, the producing or forcing that is assumed to occur between variables can never be observed directly. We cannot actually see, hear, smell, or feel that smoking is producing a change in health. Health might be changing, but it is impossible to see that it is smoking, or any other variable for that matter, that is actually producing or forcing that change. Thus, even when evidence leads to the conclusion that cause and effect have been identified, something else might actually be causing the effect. Since causality cannot be assessed directly, we must be content with the indirect evidence described above. The more consistent this indirect evidence is, and the more adequate the research methods used to obtain the evidence, the more confident we feel when inferring causality. However, causality should always be inferred with caution since no causal linkages have been definitely identified.

Other variables

Researchers seldom consider only one independent and one dependent variable in studies of causality. One reason for including additional variables is apparent from the discussion above: There might be a spurious association between independent and dependent variables, and so we must consider other variables that may be producing the association. Four other common reasons for including additional variables will be discussed in this section.

One reason is that, at least in the social and medical sciences, dependent variables are usually influenced by more than one independent variable. For example, health status might be influenced by many variables, such as smoking, use of health services, and stress. Thus, in an attempt to identify a more comprehensive set of determinants of the dependent variable, more than one independent variable is often studied.

Conversely, research may be conducted to determine if an independent variable is causally related to more than one dependent variable. We might hypothesize that smoking has a causal influence on lung cancer, shortness of breath, and emphysema. In order to examine that hypothesis, we must include all these variables in the research.

Thirdly, it is often useful to specify hypothesized relationships, that is, to determine if the relationship between independent and dependent variables is different for cases with different characteristics. For example, smokers might be more likely to have impaired health than nonsmokers, and this relationship might exist for people who are psychologically stressed but not for those who experience relatively little stress. This would specify conditions under which the hypothesis is acceptable and unacceptable. Or the relationship between smoking behavior and health impairment might appear only when another variable in addition to stress, such as sex, is included. In this case there would be no relationship when considering all people; the link would appear only when men and women were considered separately.

A final reason for considering variables in addition to the independent and dependent variables is to determine whether other variables intervene between them. An *intervening variable* accounts for a causal link between independent and dependent variables. That is, the independent variable is believed to influence the dependent variable through its impact on the intervening variable. The variable "quality of mother-infant attachment" is an intervening variable in the hypothesis that hospital and home programs (independent variables) designed to influence mother-infant relationships would increase the quality of attachment, and that this intervening variable would enhance child development (dependent variable). "Time devoted to in-depth counseling with families" would be an intervening variable if the caseload of social workers (independent variable) influences family functioning (dependent variable) through its effect on the amount of time devoted to such counseling.

Variables considered as intervening in one study may be regarded as independent or dependent in another study; variables considered independent in some studies may be identified as intervening or dependent in others, and so forth. If hypotheses and theories are adequate, variables can usually be classified readily as independent, dependent, or intervening. In causal research, however, much effort is devoted to determining whether the variables have been labeled correctly.

Reference
Blalock, Hubert M., Jr. (1964) *Causal Inferences in Nonexperimental Research.* Chapel Hill: University of North Carolina Press. Pp. 3–26.

4
Intervention Designs

Because most community health and welfare activities are intended to cause things to happen, research designs aimed at determining whether they actually do so are of special importance. *Intervention designs,* which are often used for this purpose, have two distinguishing characteristics: the independent variables are usually programs or policies, and the dependent variables are hypothesized effects of these activities. This chapter will outline the basic intervention designs and describe in general how well each provides evidence needed to infer causality.

Examples and symbols
Two examples of intervention studies will be introduced here and extended into the following sections. The hypothesis of the first should be familiar: Reducing the caseload of social workers from sixty to twenty-five families will facilitate family functioning (Wallace, 1967). To test this hypothesis, the researchers obtained detailed descriptions or "measures" of family functioning for two years of casework service among 195 multiproblem families in Chemung County, New York. One hypothesis of the second study was that an intensive mass media campaign which emphasized

prevention of unwanted pregnancies would cause a decrease in fertility (Bauman, 1975). The mass media campaign consisted of TV and radio spots and ads in newspapers and national magazines, the most expensive of which were funded at about the level of advertisements for Coca-Cola. Medium- and large-sized cities scattered across the United States received the campaign during the first half of 1971, but only the large cities will be considered in this chapter. The dependent variable of the study was the fourth-quarter fertility rate for whites (number of births to whites in October through December per 1,000 women aged fifteen to forty-four for years before, during, and after the campaign).

Many different intervention designs could be used to test the hypotheses of these two studies. Seven basic intervention designs will be presented in this chapter. Although all these designs will be illustrated by the same two examples, each of these studies actually implemented only one of the designs. In this sense, the discussion will be partly hypothetical. When the designs that were actually used are being discussed, however, this will be indicated.

As each design is presented, its strengths and weaknesses in providing evidence for inferring causality will be discussed. The basic designs, and my judgment of their relative merits in regard to causality, are summarized in Table 4.1. Each design is also represented by a diagram in Table 4.1. A box ($\square$) symbolizes the unit that does or does not receive the community health or welfare activity. When the box contains X it represents the case or cases that received the activity. In the first example study, $\boxtimes$ represents families that received services from caseworkers with the reduced load, and in the second it represents the cities that received the mass media campaign. Empty boxes are families or cities that did not receive these programs. These symbols represent the different values of the independent variables. Y indicates the dependent variable; it represents family functioning in the first example study and the fertility rate in the second. The subscript b denotes measurement of the dependent variable before the program, and a denotes measurement after that activity.

Table 4.1. Relative values of intervention designs for acquiring evidence in inferring causality

Intervention design		Association	Evidence of temporal sequence	Spurious association
Name	Diagram			
1. One group–after only	☒ Y_a	0	0	0
2. Two group–after only	☒ Y_a ☐ Y_a	+	0	0
3. One group–before after	Y_b ☒ Y_a	+	+	0
4. Two group–before after	Y_b ☒ Y_a Y_b ☐ Y_a	+	+	+
5. Two group–after only (random allocation)	☒ Y_a R ☐ Y_a	+	+	+++
6. Two group–before after (random allocation)	Y_b ☒ Y_a R Y_b ☐ Y_a	+	+	++++
7. Four group–two before and four after (random allocation)	Y_b ☒ Y_a R Y_b ☐ Y_a R ☒ Y_a R ☐ Y_a	++	++	+++++

0 = Design inadequate for obtaining evidence.

+ = Design adequate for obtaining evidence.

R = Random allocation to comparison groups.

One group–after only

In the one group–after only design, families would be exposed to the caseworker with a reduced caseload (☒), and family functioning (Y_a) would be documented later. In the second example, the fertility rate (Y_a) would be examined after the study cities had received the mass media compaign ($\boxtimes$).

Evidence of association

As we saw in the preceding chapter, the independent and dependent variables are associated if their values vary with one another. That is, the distribution of cases on the measurement scale of one variable must be different for different values of the other variable. To determine if there is an association requires that there must be cases representing more than one value of each variable; only then can we determine if the variables vary with one another. The one group–after only design provides cases with only one value for the independent variable. In the first example, it is families receiving services from social workers with a twenty-five family caseload; in the second, it is cities receiving the mass media campaign. Other values of the independent variables—families receiving service from workers with normal caseloads and cities that do not receive the campaign—are not provided by this design. Thus, when using this design, there is no way to determine if the independent and dependent variables are associated. Thus, this design cannot provide the first type of evidence for inferring causality which was discussed in Chapter 3.

Evidence that the dependent variable varied after the independent variable

The average family functioning score was 92 after the families had received services from the social workers with a reduced caseload. About a year after the mass media campaign, the cities had an average fertility rate of 17. Since the dependent variable is measured at only one point in time, we do not know if the distribution of cases on the dependent variables varied after the programs were introduced, that is, if family functioning changed after the reduction in caseload or if the fertility rate changed after the campaign. Indeed, it is not known if the dependent variables have ever changed. Since the one group–after only design does not show whether the dependent variable varied after the independent variable, it fails to provide the second type of evidence for causal inference.

Evidence that the association is not spurious
Since the one group–after only design cannot identify associations between independent and dependent variables, there is no reason to consider a possible spurious association.

The one group–after only design, although sometimes useful in describing such groups as families and cities, is unacceptable for drawing inferences about causality.

Two group–after only

If the two group–after only design were used, some caseworkers would have a reduced caseload ($\boxtimes$) and others would continue with the normal caseload of sixty families ($\square$). Both groups would be measured on family functioning after the program (Y_a). In the second example, a group of cities would receive the mass media campaign ($\boxtimes$), another group of cities would not ($\square$), and the two groups of cities would be compared with respect to fertility rates after the campaign (Y_a).

Evidence of association
This design is an advance over the one group–after only design. The addition of the group that did not receive the program provides more than one value of the independent variable. Therefore, we are able to determine whether the independent and dependent variables are associated. If the families that received workers with different caseloads differed on family functioning after the program, then we would conclude that the independent and dependent variables are associated. If the two groups were the same in family functioning after the program, then we would conclude that there is no association. Similarly, if fertility is lower or higher in campaign cities than noncampaign cities after the campaign,

then we would conclude that the independent and dependent variables are associated. If the fertility of campaign and noncampaign cities is the same, then we would infer that there is no association between the variables.

Evidence that the dependent variable varied after the independent variable

Imagine that we found an average family functioning score of 92 among families served by workers with a reduced caseload and a score of 40 for those served by workers with a normal caseload, with the higher score representing more positive family functioning. We would conclude that there is an association between independent and dependent variables, and that this association indicates better family functioning among those families whose workers had reduced caseloads. The tendency would be to conclude that the reduced caseload caused more positive family functioning. However, that would be a risky inference because we don't know if the dependent variable varied after the independent variable. Perhaps the two groups had their respective scores of 97 and 40 before as well as after the program. Under that condition, the dependent variable would not have varied after the independent variable, and it would be wrong to conclude that the reduction in caseload improved family functioning. This research design does not provide the preprogram measurement necessary to detect that possibility.

Our inability to establish whether the dependent variable varied after the independent variable can also make the conclusion of "no association" hazardous when using the two group-after only design. Suppose we found that the family functioning scores averaged 97 in both groups after the program, and from this concluded that there was no association between caseload and family functioning. It is possible that before the program the reduced caseload group had a score of zero and the normal caseload group had a score of 90. If we know that, we would conclude that the dependent variable varied after the independent variable *and* that those two variables are associated.

Because the two group–after only design does not include pre-program measures to determine whether the dependent variable varied after the independent variable, it is inadequate for providing this type of evidence relevant to inferring causality.

Evidence that the association is not spurious
There are many sources of spurious association in this design. Two are discussed below: differential selection and attrition.

Differential selection occurs when cases chosen to represent one value of the independent variable differ from those chosen to represent the other value of that variable. Suppose that for the study of caseload reduction, families with the poorest functioning were excluded from the reduced caseload group. Perhaps it was thought that those families were too seriously troubled to benefit from the program. If comparable families were not excluded from the other group, we would probably show an association between independent and dependent variables: Those receiving the program would have more favorable family functioning. But this would be a spurious association produced by differential selection rather than by the independent variable. Similar distortion can arise from self-selection. If troubled families were especially motivated to join the program of reduced caseload, and were successful in doing so, that group could rate lower than the normal caseload group and yet have improved more as a result of the program. With no preprogram measurements of the dependent variable — a feature of the two group–after only design—we cannot detect spurious associations produced by differential selection.

Differential attrition can also produce spurious associations. This occurs when cases being studies over time leave the study for some reason, if they differ from the cases that remain. If the most troubled families are more likely to drop out of the reduced caseload program than those with relatively positive family functioning, and if the normal caseload group remains the same, then this differential attrition might produce a difference between the groups after the program. With no preprogram measurements of the dependent variable in the two group–after only design, we cannot detect spurious associations produced by differential attrition.

One group—before after

With this very popular design, family functioning would have been measured before the caseload was reduced to twenty-five families (Y_b),the caseload would have been reduced to twenty-five families ($\boxtimes$), and family functioning would have been measured again after the program (Y_a). The fertility rate would have been measured before the mass media campaign (Y_b), the cities would have received the campaign ($\boxtimes$), and the fertility rate would then have been measured again (Y_a).

Evidence of association

This design allows us to determine whether an association exists between independent and dependent variables. We consider measurement of the independent variable on the group before the program as representing the "no program" value and the measurement after the program as representing the "program" value. In our first example, the study cases before the program provide one value for the independent variable (caseload of sixty families), and the group after the program provides the other value (caseload of twenty-five families). Similarly, cities before the mass media campaign provide one value of the independent variable, and the cities after the mass media campaign provide the other value. Thus, there is more than one value for the independent variable. If there is a difference in the dependent variable as measured before and after the program, then we conclude that the independent and dependent variables are associated. If there is no difference in the dependent variable before and after the program, then we conclude that there is no association.

Evidence that the dependent variable varied after the independent variable

This design is an advance over both of the designs presented above, allowing us to establish the time sequencing of independent and dependent variables. That is, this design allows us to determine whether the distribution of cases on the dependent variable was different before and after the program. If there is no difference, we conclude that the dependent variable did not vary after the independent variable, and thus that there is no causal association. Such would be the case if family functioning were 45 before and after the reduction in caseload, or if the fertility rate were 17 before and after the mass media campaign. However, if the distribution differed before and after the program—that is, if family functioning and fertility went up or down—there would be some evidence for inferring a causal relation because the dependent variable varied after the independent variable.

Evidence that the association is not spurious

Family functioning averaged 45 before the caseload was reduced, and this improved an average of 47.1 points among families whose workers had a reduced caseload. Do we conclude from this that the reduction in caseload improved family functioning?

Figure 4.1 shows the actual trends in fertility rates for the cities that received the mass media campaign during the first half of 1971. The fertility rates increased from 19 to 21 between 1968 and 1970; after the campaign, the rates declined markedly to 17 in 1971. Should we conclude from this that the campaign caused the decline in the fertility rate?

If family functioning and fertility had not changed between the times of measurement, should we conclude that there was no causal relationship between the independent and dependent variables? Suppose family functioning had declined and fertility increased. Did the programs produce the opposite of their intended effect: negative family functioning and more births?

The proper answer to all of these questions is "not necessarily." Many factors other than the programs could have accounted for the change or stability in the dependent variables. In the language of causal inference, something other than the independent variable might have produced a difference between Y_b and Y_a, or pre-

Figure 4.1. Number of Fourth-Quarter Births to Whites per 1,000 White Women Ages 15–44 (Fertility Rate) in Large Cities Which Received the Mass Media Campaign, 1968–1971.

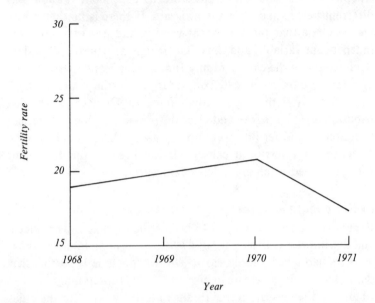

vented a difference when in fact there was a causal relationship between the variables.

Five major factors can produce spurious associations when the one group–before after design is used: 1. history; 2. maturation; 3. testing; 4. instrumentation; and 5. regression toward the mean. This research design typically handles these potential sources of spurious associations poorly, if at all, and therefore usually provides a weak basis for making judgments about causality.

History refers to influences external to the programs or policies being studied that produce change or stability in the dependent variables. After the families began dealing with workers with a reduced caseload, some family members might have secured new jobs by themselves; this change in employment, rather than the reduced caseload, enhanced family functioning. Perhaps some of the most troublesome members left the family for reasons other than the social service program, thus improving family functioning. In the cities that received the mass media campaign, other things might have occurred to cause the drop in fertility later on. Among the many possibilities are increased recruitment for family planning services by programs not related to the mass media campaign; a new directive at city health departments that all of childbearing ages be taught how to use contraceptives; and the legalization of abortions. The point here is simply that many things other than the target programs could have produced the changes in the dependent variables. If they did, to attribute the changes to the programs would obviously be an error.

Effects of history can work the other way. If funds for family planning services were reduced or the number of abortions decreased between measures of the dependent variable, fertility could have increased. A depression could occur, or the welfare system could be changed; these, rather than the reduction in caseload, could worsen family functioning between measures of the dependent variable. Thus, it might be incorrect to conclude that the programs produced negative changes. Historical events can influence dependent variables measured at different times, and the one group—before after design usually fails to control this influence.

Maturation refers to natural changes in dependent variables which occur independent of programs. The families in the reduced caseload research got older during the study. Perhaps they came to function better as a result of this natural process of aging, and this rather than the program produced higher scores on the study's measure. During the mass media campaign, the population of cities might have aged as a result of out-migration of young married couples and in-migration of older people unlikely to have babies. This rather than the mass media campaign might have produced a decline in fertility rates. For many research problems there are numerous potential sources for maturation effects.

Testing produces spurious associations that can be attributed to the preprogram measures themselves. For example, families might have scored higher on a family functioning test after the program simply as a result of their earlier testing experience. Stimulated by study questions before the program, some families might have sought counseling services or literature that were not associated with the caseworker, and these rather than the reduced caseload might have improved family functioning.

Instrumentation refers to a possible change in the measuring process before and after the program. If the same observers rated family functioning before and after the reduced caseload program, in the interim they might have become more skillful as a result of their experience with the measurement procedures. Their greater skill might have enabled them to identify more family dysfunction, producing an apparent decline in family functioning. In our second example, fertility could be lower after the program than before through a change in the boundaries for counting births—for example, if the city limits were moved. The one group–before and after design does not automatically control for instrumentation effects.

Regression toward the mean has wide relevance. Here it applies to designs, such as the one group–before after, in which measures must be repeated for the same cases. When variables are measured more than once, at least some cases will have different values for the two measures. If I complete a test to measure my mathematical aptitude in January, and again in February, chances are that I will not get the same score each time. I might get 85 percent the first time and 83 percent the second time—very close, but not identical. These differences are probably not due to actual changes—my aptitude in math is probably the same—but rather to the inherent instability of measures resulting from factors that will be discussed further in Chapter 8.

Now, if cases are selected for study because they represent extreme values of a behavior—for example, if troubled families, as indicated by our preprogram measure, are chosen to receive the reduced caseload—then as a group they will probably function better when measured again even if they are not exposed to a program. This is because most cases vary on repeated tests, and when they represent extreme values to begin with, the chances increase that the later measure will regress away from the extreme value— that is, toward the mean. Since the measures are separated by a program, there is a tendency to conclude that any difference between them is due to the program. Regression toward the mean is one of the least discussed and most often overlooked sources of spurious association in applications of the one group–before after design. It should often be offered as an alternative to the conclusion that a program or policy has had an effect, but is seldom recognized. It is especially critical for community health and welfare personnel to consider this possibility since their research is often directed toward groups with extreme values.

In summary, when the one group–before after design is used, these five factors can compete with the conclusion that a program did or did not have a causal influence on the dependent variable. In addition, differential attrition can play a role. If the most troubled families drop out of the program, then the families that remain in the study will have more positive family functioning. However, this improvement might reflect spurious rather than causal association.

The one group–before after design is preferable to those discussed earlier because it can show both the association and the time relationship between independent and dependent variables. However, it is usually unsatisfactory for drawing tenable inferences about causality because it offers so many possibilities for spurious relationships.

Two group–before after
In this research strategy, families that do (☒) and those that do

not (□) have social workers with reduced caseloads would be measured on the dependent variable "family functioning" before (Y_b) and after (Y_a) the program. This is the design actually used in our study of the influence of a mass media campaign upon fertility: The fertility rates for the cities that received the campaign (☒) and the cities that did not receive the campaign (□) were compared before and afterward.

Evidence of association

Like some of the others, this design allows us to determine whether the independent and dependent variables are associated. Figure 4.2 shows the actual results from our study of the mass media campaign. The conclusions to be drawn are quite clear: The fertility rate before and after the campaign followed very similar trends for both campaign and noncampaign cities. Thus, we conclude that there is no association between the campaign and trends in fertility rates, inferring that there is no causal relationship between these independent and dependent variables.

Evidence that the dependent variable varied after the independent variable

As in the one group–before after design, measurements of the dependent variable before and after the program allow us to determine if the dependent variable varied after the independent variable. In our study of the mass media campaign (see Figures 4.1 and 4.2), the fertility rates were different before and afterward. Even though the dependent variable varied after the independent variable, however, we inferred that the campaign was not responsible because the independent and dependent variables were not associated. This illustrates the fact that more than one type of evidence is often necessary to infer causality with confidence.

Evidence that the association is not spurious

When an association between independent and dependent variables is found using this design, and when inferring causality, it is

Figure 4.2. Number of Fourth-Quarter Births to Whites per 1,000 White Women Ages 15–44 (Fertility Rate) in Large Cities Which Did and Did Not Receive the Mass Media Campaign, 1968–1971

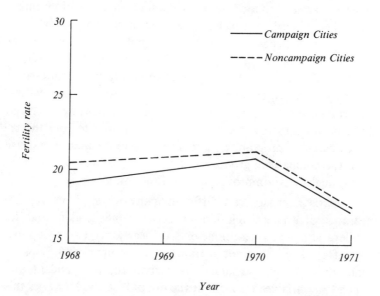

Reprinted with permission from *The Demographic Evaluation of Domestic Family Planning Programs,* Copyright 1975, Ballinger Publishing Company.

necessary to assume that the independent variable alone caused the dependent variable to vary. Sometimes this assumption is untenable.

Suppose that before the program of reduced caseload, both comparison groups had scores of 45, and that the families which received the program had an average score of 92 on the second measurement of family functioning while the other group had the same score of 45. We would be inclined to conclude that the program had a positive effect on the families that received it. Now, suppose further that the families which received the program were much more likely than those in the comparison group to have fewer than two children as a result of differential selection. If families with few children have more time to work out their problems than families with many children, and if this influences family functioning, then the number of children rather than the reduced caseload might have improved family functioning. Another possibility is that the families which received the program were older than the comparison group, matured earlier as a result of aging, and thus improved in family functioning after the program when compared with the other group. Thus, maturation rather than the program might have led to this improvement. Perhaps families that were especially motivated to join the reduced caseload program were more highly motivated to improve than the comparison group; the motivation, rather than the program, might have improved family functioning.

Comparison groups can differ in many ways, giving the appearance of a causal relationship between independent and dependent variables where none exists. Clearly, the two group–before after design does not guarantee that comparison groups remain the same on variables other than the independent and dependent variables throughout the life of a study. Nor does this design guarantee that such differences may not explain an association between independent and dependent variables. Since there are usually many other such variables, and not all are known or measured in any single study, this research design is vulnerable to spurious associations.

Nevertheless, this design is substantially better for accumulating evidence about causality than those discussed earlier. A comparison of Figures 4.1 and 4.2 shows clearly why it is preferable to the one group–before after. Inspect only the trend in fertility rates for cities that received the campaign in Figure 4.2, which is the same line shown in Figure 4.1 and is equivalent to research using the one group–before after design. Fertility increased gradually before the program and then declined markedly. From this alone, we would be inclined to conclude that there is an association between the campaign and fertility, and that the campaign caused the fertility decline. Figure 4.2, however, compares the trend for the campaign cities with the trend for the no-campaign cities and shows that the trends are nearly identical. Thus, we conclude that there is no relationship between independent and dependent variables and infer that the campaign did not cause a decline in fertility.

The two group—before after design is usually the best choice among the intervention designs discussed so far. If the comparison groups were the same on all characteristics before the program, and remained constant throughout the study except for the independent and possibly the dependent variables, then this design would be as good as any other for making inferences about causality. In fact, we are often satisfied with this strategy when we have evidence that the groups being compared are similar in various ways, especially on the dependent variable, before the program. The weakness of the design is that we can never determine whether the comparison groups are the same on all necessary characteristics throughout the life of a study.

A note on matching

We might suspect that families with different age and sex compositions differ substantially in functioning, and that if the families which do and those which do not receive the reduced caseload program differ in age and sex composition, then this factor rather than the program could explain differences in family functioning. Our research problem is to determine whether the program, not age and sex, has an effect. Thus, for each family that receives the program and is of a particular age and sex composition, we might place another with the same composition in the group that does not receive the program. When the cases have been matched in this way, any differences between the comparison groups in family functioning would not be attributable to age and sex. Whereas matching is often a valuable procedure, it certainly does not guarantee that groups are the same on all variables other than the independent one which might produce variation in the dependent variable. We cannot match on all possible variables because that would require a very large number of families.

Furthermore, we probably would not know all the variables that need to be matched. Matching by age, sex, socioeconomic status, education, and other variables can help achieve comparability of groups but it cannot guarantee comparability for all variables that might be relevant.

An introduction to random allocation

The designs discussed below, in contrast to those already presented, compare groups that are formed by *random allocation.* Random allocation means that the comparison group to which a case is assigned for study is determined by chance, so that each case has the same chance to be in any group. If there are two comparison groups, we could flip a coin, or use some analagous method, to allocate cases to values of the independent variable. If the coin turns up "heads," for instance, then the family receives the worker with the reduced caseload. If the coin shows "tails," then the family receives the worker with the normal caseload. Repeating this process with all study families yields comparison groups created by random allocation. Using our second example, the names of twenty cities are placed on separate and identical sheets of paper, folded with the names inside, placed in a hat, and mixed thoroughly. A blindfolded person selects ten sheets from the hat. These ten cities receive the mass media campaign and the rest serve as controls. When random allocation is used to create comparison groups, the one receiving the program is called the *experimental group* and the other is the *control group.*

Random allocation to experimental and control groups always provides cases that are intended to represent different values of an independent variable. Thus, associations may be indentified. In addition, random allocation allows us to assume, within calculable limits of probability to be discussed later, that the experimental and control groups were similar with respect to 1. the dependent variables at the outset of the study and 2. variables other than those considered to be independent and dependent through the life of the study. These features are important in providing evidence necessary for inferring causality.

Random allocation allows us to assume, within known limits of probability, that the groups being compared were the same on the dependent variable before the independent variable was introduced. With random allocation we assume that the families in the experimental and control groups were the same on family functioning before the program, and that before the mass media campaign the cities to be compared had the same rate of fertility. Thus, if the dependent variables are distributed differently in experimental and control groups after the program, then we can conclude that the dependent variable varied after the independent variable. If the distributions of dependent variables do not differ in experimental and control groups after the program, then we conclude that the dependent variable did not vary after the independent variable and thus infer that those variables are not related causally.

Since neither the researcher nor the cases for study chose the placement group, we have eliminated bias due to selection. Families who wanted to have a social worker with reduced caseload were not given preference for entering the experimental group. Cities with especially high rates of fertility were not given the option to receive the mass media campaign. The researchers were not permitted to assign the most highly motivated families to workers with reduced caseloads and did not give preference to cities with the best family planning services. By definition, successful random allocation eliminates bias due to selection.

Random allocation also helps ensure that outside influences are equally distributed between the experimental and control groups, eliminating the influence of history. Families might be exposed to activities other than reduced caseload, and these might produce a change in family function. However, random allocation tends to increase the chances that these activities would be distributed randomly between the groups being compared, canceling out their influence on the dependent variable after the program. We said earlier that cities which received the mass media campaign might have been influenced by a change in abortion laws or by new family planning services, and that these events rather than the mass media campaign influenced fertility. This would concern us if such changes occurred differently in cities that did or did not receive the campaign. Random allocation would increase the chances that these and other effects of history would be distributed evenly among both groups of cities, so that the dependent variable after the program would not be affected by history.

Random allocation also helps equalize maturation across experimental and control groups. The families got older during the study, and the process of maturation might have changed their functioning naturally. Random allocation helps ensure that the families receiving workers with reduced and normal caseload had similar natural maturation processes throughout the study, so that differences in the dependent variable between experimental and control groups after the study would be due to something other than maturation.

With regression toward the mean, random allocation again helps us ensure that, if regression occurs, it does so equally in experimental and control groups. Since the dependent variable was distributed similarly in the experimental and control groups before the program, a between-group difference in the dependent variable after the program would not be attributable to regression toward the mean. There may be extreme values for the dependent variable before the program, but random allocation produces comparison groups with equal rates. Thus, if regression occurs, the chances are that it will occur at an equal rate for both groups.

It is also safe to assume that any influence of instrumentation or testing would be randomly distributed between experimental and control groups. If the observers of family functioning became more skillful in observing the experimental group, random allocation would help ensure similar changes in skill vis-à-vis the control group

In summary, random allocation gives us more confidence that the groups being compared are similar, and therefore that these other variables do not account for relationships between independent and dependent variables. In other words, it helps eliminate the possibility that other variables are producing a spurious association, thus making it more certain that a relationship between the independent and dependent variables is causal.

Since we are dealing with probabilities, however, there is always a chance that comparison groups will differ on relevant variables in ways that lead to incorrect conclusions about causal relationships, even when random allocation has been used. How good are our chances that random allocation will create acceptably similar comparison groups? Suppose we have applied appropriate tests of statistical significance (see Chapter 10), using the .05 significance level to decide if the groups were different on any variable except the independent variable. We would be wrong only 5 times in 100 if we concluded that there was no difference between the groups on the variable. Those are pretty good odds. Among 50 variables not related to one another, there will be a statistically significant difference between experimental and control groups for 2 or 3 of the 50 variables at the .05 significance level. Those are quite good odds that our comparison groups are similar on most variables other than the independent and dependent variables before the program. Although random allocation does not certify that comparison groups are so evenly matched that we can make definitive conclusions about causality, it does permit us to calculate the odds that our inferences will be correct and the odds are in our favor.

Two group–after only with random allocation

The important difference between this design and the two group–after only design is that random allocation has been added. Thus, in this design, families would be allocated randomly to the groups which did (☒) or did not (☐) receive social workers with reduced caseloads.

The major limitation of this design, when compared with those presented below, is that since random allocation does not guarantee identical experimental and control groups on all variables except the independent variable, and since the dependent and other variables are not measured before the program starts, we do not know for certain that the experimental and control groups are comparable on these variables before the experiment. The designs discussed below take this into account.

Two group—before after with random allocation

This design is identical to the preceding one except that the dependent variable would also be measured before the program. The families would be measured on family functioning before the program began, allocated randomly to experimental and control groups, and measured again on the dependent variable some time after the program was initiated. This design most closely resembles the one that was actually used in the study of reduced caseload. The advantage of this design over the two group—after only with random allocation is that since random allocation does not guarantee identical comparison groups, measurement of the dependent and other variables before the program allows us to determine systematically how well random allocation worked—that is, how comparable the experimental and comparison groups were.

The potentially contaminating effects of history, maturation, selection, statistical regression, testing, and instrumentation are controlled the same way as in the two group—after only design with random allocation. That is, if random allocation has worked, the comparison groups are influenced the same way by these factors. Thus, any change in the dependent variable which is different for experimental and control groups can be attributed to something other than those factors.

All this sounds good, and it should, but as we have seen, random allocation is not perfect. If we are unlucky, the experimental and control groups might be different on some variable other than the independent variable, perhaps an unmeasured one that produces variation in the dependent variable. Though the design is efficient, we must still only infer causality, resisting the temptation to announce our findings with complete certainty.

Moreover, we must resist overgeneralization. Although we would prefer to generalize our results to different populations at different times, that step cannot be taken automatically and must always be made with qualification. One reason is that the program in combination with something else might have been producing variation in the dependent variable which would not have occurred in absence of the "something else." Thus, if we reintroduce the program and the other thing is not present, the results might be different.

Consider first the possibility that testing is that other thing. Imagine the families had been given an in-depth interview before the reduced caseload program was introduced and asked to identify the positive and negative features of their family functioning. That interview might have sensitized the families to their problems and, in combination with the reduced caseload program, might have changed their functioning. The program without the pre-program interview might have produced no change.

Historical factors in combination with the program could also have produced results that would have been different if history had changed. If the mass media program had been introduced at a time when family planning was an especially popular notion, it might have been the social climate plus the mass media program that produced an association between the campaign and a decline in fertility. If the campaign had been introduced at another time, when reducing fertility was less popular, the campaign might have had no effect on behavior. Thus, the extent to which we can generalize our findings depends, in part, on the interaction between the independent variable and history.

These considerations on generalizability also apply to intervention designs without random allocation. Unfortunately, with the exception to be noted in the final design discussed below, no research designs have been developed that systematically guard against these effects of interaction. To control the effects of the interaction between the independent variable and history, we must repeat the study under situations that reflect different histories rather than use a different design to control these effects.

Four group–two before and four after with random allocation
If this design were applied to the study of family functioning, at

least four groups would be needed. Two of them would be measured for the dependent variable before the program and two would not. All groups would be measured for the dependent variable after the program. In the spirit of true experimentation, the groups would be formed by random allocation. This design is composed of the two intervention designs discussed above: the two group–before after with random allocation and the two group–after only with random allocation. Thus, it provides two tests of hypotheses related to associations between independent and dependent variables through the use of two different designs.

The four group–two before and four after design has the added advantage that the possible effects of testing and the interaction of testing with the program can be assessed. To test for these effects, the two groups that receive the program are compared with respect to the dependent variable after the program, and the two groups that did not receive the program are compared with respect to the dependent variable after the program. If there are no differences for these comparisons, then it is concluded that there are no effects due to testing or the interaction between the testing and the program. If there are differences in the dependent variables for these comparisons, then it must be concluded that there might be testing or interaction effects. Because this design has all the strengths of the designs with random allocation which we have discussed, and also allows assessment for the influence of testing, it is often the most satisfactory design for providing evidence relevant to inferring causality.

Several other considerations

As we have seen, regardless of study design, cases are not immune from all factors that might influence the dependent variable. Thus, making a virtue of necessity, some studies aim to measure the influence of other factors.

Other independent variables could be added to any of the designs discussed above. We might wish to know whether providing income supplements is better than a reduction in caseload for enhancing family functioning. Or we might want to determine if increasing subsidized family planning services influences fertility more than a mass media campaign. This could be done by adding groups that received income supplements or subsidized family planning services to the designs presented above.

Although this chapter has focused on studies using one dependent variable, most programs and policies have multiple objectives, so that dependent variables are often added to intervention designs. For example, the program of reduced caseload might also focus on reduction of psychological stress, and the mass media campaign might aim to reduce perinatal mortality. Measures of these variables could then be incorporated into the studies. In the same way, program influence on intervening variables can be assessed by adding relevant measures.

Another intervention strategy is to compare groups that are exposed to different programs or policies, excluding from study groups that were not exposed. For example, rather than assign families to experimental and control groups in the manner described thus far, we would allocate families randomly to receive either social workers with a reduced caseload or income supplements. Families that receive neither program are excluded from study. Our research question is whether the two programs influence family functioning differently. If the two groups exhibit different trends, then we infer that the programs influenced family functioning differently. Note that we do not conclude that the program exhibiting the least influence did not influence family functioning, or that its influence was modest; these inferences would require a control group which received neither program. If the groups representing different programs have similar trends in family functioning, then we infer that the programs had no differential influence. However, we do not infer that the programs had no influence: Both programs could be having profound but comparable influences on family functioning which cannot be assessed adequately because the nonprogram group was excluded. These designs can be very valuable for testing hypotheses about the comparative effects of different programs or policies. Their adequacy for this purpose is generally analagous to that of the basic intervention designs they use.

Designs which include both program groups and no-program groups sometimes risk diffusion between experimental and control groups. That is, a program may appear to have had no effect because the trends in dependent variables are the same across comparison groups; actually the nonprogram group has received the program inadvertently. For example, the mass media campaign might be accidentally introduced in a no-campaign city, or families receiving the reduced caseload program pass on what they have learned to the control families. In many intervention studies, care must be taken to avoid diffusion and to assess the possibility of diffusion effects.

For a thorough but concise discussion of intervention research designs, the excellent book by Campbell and Stanley (1963) is recommended.

A comment on evaluation

Program and policy evaluation is an important activity in community health and welfare. *Outcome evaluation* is the process of determining whether program and policy goals or objectives have been achieved. This often entails a systematic search for explanation of program success or failure. Obviously, the search relates to causality: Did the programs actually cause their intended effects? The intervention designs presented here are very useful in addressing this question.

But the most trustworthy designs are not necessarily the most popular. Program administrators and others frequently evaluate programs by examining dependent variables after the programs have been going for a while. Sometimes they measure the degree of objective achievement (dependent variable) before the program began and compare that with the measure after the program has been operating for a period or has ended. The reason for these studies, of course, is to determine if program objectives are being achieved. Note that the two approaches are analogous to the first two designs presented above: one group–after only and one group–before after. Recall the multiple explanations that compete with causal inferences when these designs are used. Clearly, we should not automatically accept the conclusions when these popular ways of evaluating outcomes of programs and policies are used.

Suchmann (1967) and Weiss (1972) consider in greater detail the application of intervention designs in evaluation research.

References

Bauman, Karl E. (1975) "An Experimental Design for Family Planning Program Evaluation." In *The Demographic Evaluation of Domestic Family Planning Programs,* edited by J. Richard Udry and Earl E. Huyck. Cambridge, Mass.: Ballinger. Pp. 67–79.

Campbell, Donald T.; and Stanley, Julian C. (1963) *Experimental and Quasi-Experimental Designs for Research.* Chicago: Rand McNally.

Suchmann, Edward A. (1967) *Evaluative Research.* New York: Russell Sage Foundation. Pp. 91–114.

Wallace, David (1967) "The Chemung County Evaluation of Casework Service to Dependent Multiproblem Families: Another Problem Outcome." *Social Service Review* 41:379–89.

Weiss, Carol H. (1972) *Evaluation Research: Methods for Assessing Program Effectiveness.* Englewood Cliffs, N.J.: Prentice-Hall. Pp. 60–91.

5
Nonintervention Designs

As suggested in the preceding chapter, a research design is a combination of the way in which study groups are formed and the timing for measurement of the independent and dependent variables. The purpose of nonintervention research designs, like that of intervention designs, is to provide evidence necessary for inferring causality. The distinguishing characteristic of nonintervention designs, when compared with intervention designs, is that the independent variables do not directly reflect programs or policies. Examples of hypotheses which have been tested by use of nonintervention designs are listed below. For each hypothesis, either the independent variable or its values is in italics.

1. *Psychologically stressed* members of a prepaid group medical practice make more visits to the practice than those who are *not psychologically stressed* (Tessler, Mechanic, and Dimond, 1976).
2. The use of illegal drugs by high school students is determined by the *use of illegal drugs by their peers* (Kandel, 1973).
3. *Smokers* have lower birth weight babies than *nonsmokers* (Frazier, 1966; Yerushalmy, 1971).
4. *Females* are more likely than *males* to have chronic conditions (Verbrugge, 1976).

Hypotheses tested by nonintervention designs are often fundamental to programs and policies even though these may not be mentioned in the hypotheses. The assumption that young people use illegal drugs because their peers use them is part of the rationale for drug education programs in some schools that focus on the dynamics of peer groups. It also explains why some parents try to monitor their children's friends. The presumed causal connection between smoking and birth weight is basic to many different programs and policies designed to reduce smoking, including the health warning on cigarette packages and mass media and school education programs.

If the implied causal relationships do not exist, then the programs and policies that stem from the assumptions must be justified in other ways. If these relationships are not causal then programs and policies aimed at the supposedly independent variables will probably not have the intended effects unless the unknown causal variables are accidentally influenced in the process. If the use of illegal drugs is caused by boredom rather than the behavior of peer groups, then a program to reduce drug use would presumably succeed better if it reduced boredom than if it influenced peer group behavior. Programs and policies are most likely to influence dependent variables if they have an impact on their independent variables.

Three basic nonintervention designs are commonly used in community health and welfare research. They will be outlined below, and their adequacy for inferring causality will be discussed.

Cross-sectional design
In this popular nonintervention design, information is gathered at one time for the cases being studied. Tessler, Mechanic, and Dimond (1976), for instance, conducted household interviews with 506 members of a prepaid goup medical practice in studying the relationship between psychological stress and use of the practice. Kandel (1973) administered questionnaires to 1,112 high school

students and their peers to study peer group influence on the use
of marijuana.

Evidence of association

It can be determined if the independent and dependent variables
are associated when using a cross-sectional design if there are
enough cases for the values of each variable being studied. If
enrollees of the prepaid group medical practice represent different
degrees of stress, and they visit the practice with varying frequen-
cies, then it can be determined if an association exists between
stress and the frequency of visits. In general, we can determine if
associations exist as hypothesized if the values of all variables are
represented by study cases. If some values of the independent or
dependent variables are not represented, then we cannot ascertain
if an association exists. We could not find out if sex and number
of chronic conditions were linked by studying only one sex, or if
all cases had the same number of chronic conditions.

Since there were enough cases for all values of each variable in
the studies that tested the four hypotheses listed on page 50 it was
possible to determine if the associations specified by the hypotheses existed. Each hypothesis was confirmed. Stressed patients
made more visits to the practice than those who were not stressed.
A total of 48 percent of the high school students whose friends
had used marijuana sixty or more times used marijuana themselves, compared to 2 percent of those whose friends had never
used marijuana. Also, 12 percent of the smokers had babies with
low birth weight, compared to 7 percent of the nonsmokers. In a
cross-sectional survey of the U.S. population, women were more
likely than men to report chronic conditions.

Evidence that the dependent variable varied after the independent variable

There is a temptation to conclude that the associations described
above are causal. This may not be so. Among other things, we do
not know if the dependent variable varied after the independent
variable. Perhaps stress was the effect rather than the cause of

visits to the medical practice. Medical settings are not always pleasant for the patient, and the diagnoses they receive can be stressful. Young people may begin using marijuana when they are alone, or with persons other than peers, and then join peer groups that use marijuana or introduce marijuana to their peers. Thus, a person's use of marijuana might cause the formation of peer groups of marijuana smokers rather than the reverse. The associations as hypothesized and reflected by the data would exist, but the conclusion that the independent variable had a causal influence on the dependent variable would be incorrect. Clearly, we need evidence about the time sequence of the variables labeled as independent and dependent. Did the dependent variable vary after the independent variable? If so, our inference that the independent variable caused the dependent variable to change gains credence.

When using a cross-sectional design, a presumably simple way to assess the time sequence of variables is to ask subjects about it. We could ask women if they began smoking before or after they had their babies, or we could obtain a detailed history of smoking behavior before, during, and after pregnancy. We could ask subjects to indicate when they became stressed, and then determine if stress began before or after the decision to visit the practice. If we could determine which variables varied first, we might be able to label them correctly as independent and dependent variables. But this approach has limitations. It relies on the subject's memory, and few of us have infallible memories. When attitudes or other psychological variables are involved, the subtlety of their change may make it difficult or impossible for people to ascertain the time sequence. For example, many subjects may not know exactly when they became stressed because the stress developed over a long period of time. We usually have more faith in reports of events which do not go too far back into history or which are relatively major or concrete. Examples include age at marriage, birth date of child, and year of change in residence or job.

Identifying the time sequence for some variables is automatic. That is, for some associations it is logical to consider certain variables independent and others dependent. The relationship between sex and morbidity is a good example. It does not make sense to reason that whether subjects are male or female was established, or varied, after a chronic condition was acquired. Therefore, we can assume with confidence that if there is a causal association between sex and chronic conditions, it is in the direction of sex leading to chronic conditions rather than the reverse. If causal relationships are hypothesized between race and attitude toward social services, age and the frequency of nurse-patient interaction, or socioeconomic status and the quality of mother-infant attachment, it is safe to assume that race, age, and sex are the independent variables in these hypotheses. Further, if independent and dependent variables are related, then the dependent variable varied after the independent variable.

Evidence that the association is not spurious

There are typically many sources for spurious association in all nonintervention study designs. If research with a cross-sectional design produced evidence that smoking and birth weight are associated, and that birth weight varies after smoking, we should still be cautious about inferring causality. Perhaps younger women are more likely to smoke prior to conception than older women and are more likely to have low birth weight babies for reasons other than smoking. Maybe younger women have less nutritious diets or immature physiques, and these rather than smoking influence birth weight. The relationship between smoking and birth weight might then be attributable to the common association of age with smoking, and nutrition and physical maturity with age, but we would consider it a spurious association because it negates the hypothesis that smoking causes low birth weight.

When using a cross-sectional design, one strategy for identifying spurious associations is to gather data for variables which might produce spurious associations and use appropriate analysis techniques, such as those we discuss in Chapters 9 and 10, to determine whether they actually had that effect. Even when this is done, however, we cannot be certain that all variables which might be producing a spurious association have been included. Some variables may be unknown, or costs may have precluded gathering information for all variables considered important.

Trend design

In a cross-sectional study, data are collected at one point in time. In a trend design, which documents changes in variables, two or more cross-sectional designs are implemented at different times. Different subjects are usually contacted when data are collected at different times. If some of the cases are the same, then in contrast to the panel design discussed in the next section, in a trend study there is no attempt to link the information they provided at different times.

In causal research, one trend study is often used in conjunction with one or more others. Higgins (1976) studied trends in deaths from malignancy in the respiratory system between 1940 and 1970, together with information on smoking behavior from household interviews conducted several times between 1955 and 1970, in an effort to gather additional evidence on whether cigarette smoking is causally related to death from lung cancer.

Evidence of association

Trend studies can be used to determine if independent and dependent variables are associated. Higgins concluded that lung cancer and smoking behavior were linked when he observed that death rates from lung cancer increased over the same period that an increasing proportion of the population smoked cigarettes. He would have concluded that there was no association between the two variables if only one of them had changed.

Evidence that the dependent variable varied after the independent variable

Trend studies can provide clear evidence regarding the time sequence of variables if information is gathered at times when one of the variables changed after the other. This can be a distinct advantage over the cross-sectional design for testing some hypotheses. For example, if we conducted five surveys of smoking behavior and lung cancer, and found that a marked increase in smoking was followed by an increase in deaths from lung cancer, then we would have such evidence. From a practical standpoint, we are often unable to afford data collection at short enough intervals to pinpoint exactly when some variables begin to change and whether it is before or after others. Moreover, variables sometimes change gradually so that the marked changes necessary to determine the time relationship between independent and dependent variables are not always present. However, the trend design can be applied to vital, census, and other data that are collected routinely and periodically, and sometimes the time sequence of variables can be identified.

Evidence that the association is not spurious

Innumerable variables can produce a spurious association between independent and dependent variables in trend studies. Indeed, the competing explanations to causality discussed in Chapter 4—selection, history, maturation, testing, instrumentation, and statistical regression—are all applicable to this design. Like cross-sectional studies, therefore, trend studies must attempt to obtain information on the other variables that might produce a spurious association between those considered as independent and dependent, and then account for them during analysis. As with any other research design, however, these variables may be numerous and some may be unknown.

Panel design

In the panel design, information is gathered from the *same* cases at two or more different times, and the different sets of data are linked by case. For instance, we might obtain information on the smoking behavior of a group of women while they are pregnant, and later determine the birth weight of their babies. The study of stress and use of a prepaid group medical practice by Tessler and his colleagues (1976) included a panel as well as a cross-sectional design. They measured the stress of people entering the program during household interviews in the summer of 1973 and then examined their records at the practice to document the use of health services during the year after the interview. Thus, for each subject they were able to correlate stress level with subsequent use of the service.

Evidence of association

Panel design studies provide sufficient evidence to determine whether independent and dependent variables are associated if there are enough cases distributed among values of the variables. This was true in the study of enrollees in the prepaid group medical practice: There were subjects with different degrees of stress, and within the year some used the service while others did not. The researchers would not have been able to infer causality if there were few or no stressed subjects, if all subjects were stressed, or if either all or none of the subjects had visited the practice.

Both trend and panel designs are longitudinal; that is, data are gathered more than once. However, if some of the same cases give information at different times in a study using a trend design, there is no linkage between the different sets of data, whereas there is in panel studies. This is fundamental to the nature of associations identified by trend and panel designs. Suppose the study hypothesis is that smokers are more likely to die from lung cancer than nonsmokers. To test this hypothesis, a study using the trend design might compare the trends in the percentages who smoke and the probabilities of death from lung cancer. However, even if the variables were linked as hypothesized—both smoking and deaths increased in the population—this evidence alone would not tell us if smokers are more likely to die from lung cancer than nonsmokers. Rather, we only know that over time the variables vary with one another. The increase in lung cancer may be entirely attributable to the nonsmokers, but the trend study as described would not necessarily tell us so. In contrast, a panel study would separate the probability of dying from lung cancer for smokers and nonsmokers, thus providing a more direct test of the hypothesis. Panel studies often provide more adequate evidence of causality than trend studies.

Evidence that the dependent variable varied after the independent variable

An advantage of the panel design over other nonintervention designs is that it is often more effective in clarifying the time relationship between variables. As we saw with the trend design, the intervals between data collection might be too great to allow us to observe one variable changing after the other. Using annual surveys to document smoking behavior and lung cancer, for example, we might find that both variables have changed between data collection points. This makes it impossible to determine which variable changed after the other. In contrast, the panel design makes it possible to pinpoint more exactly the evidence that change in one variable occurred before or after the other. For example, a panel study might begin with a group of subjects known to be free of lung cancer. Data are collected from this group periodically, and some contract lung cancer. If there is a difference in the probability of acquiring lung cancer between smokers and nonsmokers, then the dependent variable (lung cancer) varied or changed after the smoking behavior.

If they were less expensive and time-consuming, panels would probably be used much more often. Because the panel design often pinpoints the time relationship between independent and dependent variables more precisely than other nonintervention designs, it provides stronger evidence for inferring causality.

Evidence that the association is not spurious

Panel studies are not immune to spurious associations. Suppose our study finds that women who began smoking before conception were more likely to have low birth weight babies than nonsmokers. Perhaps the women who began smoking have other characteristics that changed and are also associated with having a low birth weight baby. For instance, they might have begun drinking alcohol or become more anxious. If these variables explain why smoking and birth weight are associated, their causal role could be obscured by their association with smoking behavior.

One's preconceptions in any research study may make it easy to overlook such possibilities. Tessler and his colleagues recognized that although use of the group medical practice varied after stress, other variables might make this a spurious association. For example, older people may be more likely to be stressed and may also be more likely to use a group practice. Through refined analyses the researchers explored the possibility of spurious associations with fourteen sociodemographic, attitudinal, and health status variables. They concluded that the association was not produced spuriously by these variables, and this strengthened their inference that stress increased use of the practice.

One problem with panel designs, when compared with cross-sectional and trend designs, is that since data must be gathered from the same subjects more than once, there is likely to be attrition of the study group. For example, if we need to gather data from our cases two or more times over a five-year period, then some are likely to move during that period and will be lost to study because they cannot be located. Generally, the less the sample attrition the more confidence we have in the findings from panel studies.

Attrition is more important in testing some hypotheses than others. If people without psychological stress are more likely to move from an area within a year than those with stress, then the association between stress and clinic use might be due to migration rather than stress. This differential attrition within the study population, by depleting the without-stress group, could give rise to a spurious association between stress and clinic use. On the other hand, if we experienced attrition in a panel study on smoking and birth weight but were unable to identify ways that attrition could influence the possible conclusions, there would not be much reason for concern. When using panel designs special efforts should be make to keep attrition at a minimum, but some degree of attrition has to be tolerated in order to take advantage of the design. Whenever possible, data should be gathered and analyzed to assess the possiblity of attrition effects.

Additional thoughts on nonintervention designs

Basic nonintervention designs can be varied by forming the comparisons groups through disproportionate selection of cases according to values of the independent or dependent variables. This is useful when cases are relatively rare for one or more values of the variables and it is necessary to have enough cases representing all values. For example, if we select 100 mothers who delivered a baby to study the relationship between smoking and birth weight, and 5 percent of the babies had low birth weight, we will have only 5 mothers with low birth weight babies to compare with 95 mothers with normal birth weight babies. If we decided that at least 50 mothers with low birth weight babies were needed, we would have to obtain information from 1,000 mothers to attain that number. Suppose funds are available to study only 100 mothers. We could first examine birth records to identify 50 low birth weight babies and 50 normal birth weight babies and then obtain information on the smoking behavior of their mothers. The procedures for gathering evidence relevant to inferring causality when one adopts this strategy, as well as the limitations, are much the same as for the cross-sectional and panel designs described above.

In attempting to control for spurious associations in nonintervention designs, "matching" is a commonly used method. Suppose we suspect that younger women are more likely to smoke than older women, that younger women are more likely to have a low birth weight baby than older women, and that we do not want a difference in age between groups who do and do not smoke to explain an association between smoking and birth weight. For each woman who smokes and is of a particular age, we could select another woman of the same age who does not smoke until we have enough cases for study. Thus, the groups of smokers and nonsmokers will have the same age distributions, and any differences in birth weight between the groups will not be attributable to this variable. This does not guarantee that cases will be identical for all variables which might produce a spurious association, but by using this procedure we can assure that several of the more critical variables are not producing spurious associations.

Another way to assure that key variables are not producing spurious associations when using nonintervention designs is to narrow the study group in terms of the variable which might cause a spurious association. For example, if it is suspected that age might produce a spurious association between smoking behavior and birth weight, only subjects of a particular age are studied— say, those twenty-two years old. Although this limits the age group to which the findings can be generalized, if an association exists it can be concluded it is not produced spuriously by age.

All of our examples have used individuals as the unit of analysis, but nonintervention designs are often applied to other units, such as neighborhoods, cities, clinics, and countries. For example, cities might be compared according to median family income and utilization of family planning services in an attempt to determine if income has an influence on use of the services. Or clinics in urban and rural areas might be compared to determine if location influences attitudes toward services. In general, the same procedures are used and the same limitations are confronted, whether individuals or other entities are the units of analysis.

The studies in our simplified examples have addressed one independent and one dependent variable at a time, but nonintervention designs are often used to determine whether more than one independent variable has a causal influence on one or more dependent variables. For example, a onetime survey might be used to determine if eating habits, life style, and smoking may be causally related to birth weight. The addition of these variables is a direct extension of the principles discussed above.

In some research using nonintervention designs, critical values of the independent or dependent variables are not represented by cases but causal inferences are made anyway. For example, it might be observed that 14 percent of the offspring of a sample of smoking mothers had low birth weight. Or, it might be found that 60 percent of the people who had visited their prepaid group practice were psychologically stressed. Conclusions from clinical observations often follow this model. This design is analagous to the one group–after only intervention design discussed in Chapter 4, and carries with it all the limitations already discussed for that design. Since it is impossible to determine if an association between independent and dependent variables exists in these circumstances, causal inferences are extremely risky.

Nonintervention and intervention research designs have common functions. Basically, both designs are used to obtain information necessary to test causal hypotheses. The methods to be discussed in later chapters—sampling, measurement, and analysis—are generally applicable to both intervention and nonintervention research designs.

References

Frazier, Todd M. (1966) "Cigarette Smoking and Birth Weight: A Review of the Baltimore City Study." In *Research Methodology and Needs in Perinatal Studies,* edited by Sidney S. Chipman et al. Springfield: Charles C. Thomas. Pp. 70–87.

Higgins, Ian T. (1976) "Commentary." *American Journal of Public Health* 66:159–161.

Kandel, Denise (1973) "Adolescent Marijuana Use: Role of Parents and Peers." *Science* 181:1067–70.

Tessler, Richard; Mechanic, David; and Dimond, Margaret (1976) "The Effect of Psychological Distress on Physician Utilization: A Prospective Study." *Journal of Health and Social Behavior* 17:353–64.

Verbrugge, Lois M. (1976) "Females and Illness: Recent Trends in Sex Differences in the United States." *Journal of Health and Social Behavior* 17:387–403.

Yerushalmy, J. (1971) "The Relationship of Parents' Cigarette Smoking to Outcome of Pregnancy—Implications as to the Problem of Inferring Causation from Observed Associations." *American Journal of Epidemiology* 93:443–55.

6

Descriptive Research

Thus far we have emphasized research designed to make causal inferences. However, much of the research relevant to community health and welfare is done to provide descriptive information. Such studies, which are called *descriptive research,* include inventories of health facilities, the documentation of operating expenses of welfare programs, the determination of how social service personnel distribute their time among activities, and the identification of the number of persons in need of a service. Other questions that might be addressed by descriptive research are:

1. What percentage of women consider their gynecologist insensitive, cold, disrespectful, or vulgar?
2. What percentage of patients who receive organized family planning services also receive other public assistance?
3. Are the following maternal characteristics associated with perinatal death: marital status, age, country of origin, social class, obstetric history, parity, disease during pregnancy, and height?
4. Did the proportion of American children aged one to four who were immunized for polio increase between 1965 and 1975?

This chapter is relatively brief; descriptive studies rely more upon procedures to be considered in the following chapters than upon their designs per se.

The purpose of descriptive research and selected examples

The purpose of descriptive research is to identify characteristics of groups of persons or other entities such as countries, cities, or clinics. That is, the goal is to establish the distribution of cases according to the values of the variables under study. Haar, Halitsky, and Stricker (1977), for example, studied attitudes toward gynecologists by having 409 women complete questionnaires in gynecologists' offices located in Queens and Nassau County, New York. Among other things, they asked these patients to respond to a checklist of favorable and unfavorable adjectives applied to their gynecologists. When they distributed the cases according to the adjectives which were checked, the researchers found that 7 percent had chosen the negative adjectives "insensitive," "cold," or "vulgar." These choices, of course, described the attitudes of patients toward their gynecologists. Similarly, as part of the national reporting system for organized family planning services in the United States, consumers of those services were classified as to whether they had received other public assistance. A tally of this information revealed that 16 percent of the clients in 1975 were receiving other public assistance along with the family planning services (The Alan Guttmacher Institute, 1976).

Some descriptive studies examine associations among variables for reasons other than inferring causality. Haeri, South, and Naldrett (1974) studied the relationships between characteristics of pregnant women and whether the fetus survived the perinatal period. They did this by obtaining information on the background of 7,912 women who ended a pregnancy in 1969 and 1971 and relating such variables as marital status, age, and socioeconomic status to the survival status of the fetus. Their objective was to determine if these variables were related to survival status of the fetus so that high-risk pregnancies could be identified. They were not interested in testing the hypothesis that the variables were causally related.

Another example of descriptive research conducted to identify associations is the annual survey of immunization status conducted by the U.S. Center for Disease Control (1976). These surveys, conducted among households considered to represent the U.S. population, demonstrated that between 1965 and 1975 the proportion of children aged one to four adequately protected from polio by vaccination declined. The purpose was to view the association between year and immunization status for that age group, but the goal was not to determine if the year caused immunization status or if immunization status caused the year.

On the importance of descriptive research

Descriptive research can be quite important in community health and welfare activities. That most consumers approve of their gynecologists is reassuring and conflicts with the impressions of some people. That so few of those receiving family planning services were receiving other public assistance at the same time is relevant to the U.S. policy that the services are to be directed at those least able to afford private services. Perhaps these services are being received by only a small portion of the intended group. That immunization for polio is decreasing might signal the need for a change in policies and programs which could reverse that trend.

Comparison of descriptive and causal research

Descriptive and causal studies have many common features. Both depend upon carefully specified research hypotheses, and both can involve either single or repeated data collections. In the studies of attitudes toward gynecologists, welfare status of recipients of organized family planning, and relationships between maternal background and perinatal mortality, data were collected at one time. The survey of immunization status required several data collections. Descriptive and causal studies share the need for appropriate measurement, sampling, and analysis strategies, which will be discussed in the following chapters.

Many research efforts include both descriptive and causal components. Part of the study of attitudes toward gynecologists, for instance, aimed to identify variables which cause the attitudes. Separate descriptive studies can be used in combination to make causal inferences. The relationship between smoking behavior and lung cancer discussed in Chapter 5 is a nonintervention causal study composed of two descriptive studies: changes in smoking behavior and lung cancer incidence over time. Considered separately, those studies are descriptive; when combined to test a possible causal relation, they constitute causal research.

The difference between the purposes of descriptive and causal research is obvious: The former describes, while the latter attempts to determine if causal inferences are reasonable. The design of causal research is much more complex than that of descriptive research. Many descriptive studies do not seek associations among variables. In those that do, the time sequences among variables is unimportant. Indeed, in descriptive research it is unnecessary to distinguish among independent, intervening, and dependent variables since causal links are not hypothesized. For the same reason, there is no need to be concerned with the possibility of spurious association. That the design of descriptive research is less complex than that of causal research does not mean that it is simple. In descriptive research one must still take care to choose cases properly for study, to be accurate in allocating cases according to values of variables, and to use appropriate analysis strategies. These procedures, which are discussed in the following chapters, can become quite complex.

On causal inferences from descriptive research

Mistakenly, causal inferences are sometimes drawn from individual descriptive studies. For example, it might be concluded from knowledge of attitudes alone that the personality of the gynecologists or the physical environment of the examination room contribute to the low frequency of unfavorable attitudes among the patients. Such inferences are unsound when descriptive research designs are used to test causal hypotheses. If causal inferences are to be made from research, the intervention or nonintervention designs that will provide the necessary evidence should be used.

References

The Alan Guttmacher Institute (1976) "Organized Family Planning Services in the United States: FY 1975." *Family Planning Perspectives* 8:269–74.

Haar, Esther; Halitsky, Victor; and Stricker, George (1977) "Parents' Attitudes toward Gynecologic Examination and the Gynecologists." *Medical Care* 15:787–95.

Haeri, A. D.; South, Joanna; and Naldrett, Janet (1974) "A Scoring System for Identifying Pregnant Patients with a High Risk of Perinatal Mortality." *The Journal of Obstetrics and Gynecology of the British Commonwealth* 81:535–38.

United States Center for Disease Control (1976) "Immunization Status for Children 1–4 Years of Age, 1965–1975." *United States Immunization Survey: 1975.* Atlanta: U.S. Department of Health, Education, and Welfare. HEW Publication No. (CDC 76–8221). Pp. 3–8.

7

Samples and Populations

A *population* is the aggregate of all cases to which research findings are generalized. All residents in a country, all social service recipients processed by an agency in April 1978, all women who delivered babies in New York City in that year, or all cities in the United States with more than 300,000 inhabitants would be considered populations if those aggregates were to be learned about through research. A *sample* is a portion of a population selected for study. Samples might be studied which contain 10 percent of the country's residents, half of an agency's social service recipients, 100 of the women who delivered babies in New York City, or 25 of the cities with more than 300,000 inhabitants.

In descriptive and causal research, samples are usually studied to learn about their populations. If it were economically feasible, information would be obtained from all members of populations. But the populations are often large, and research costs increase with the number of cases studied. Costs include such things as (1) hiring, training, supervising, and paying personnel to gather and process data; (2) printing the necessary forms, interview schedules, or questionnaires; (3) analyzing the data; and (4) identifying cases for study. These and other expenses often preclude the study of all cases in a population.

Excellent treatments of sampling are available in the books by Cochran (1977), Kish (1965), and Stuart (1968), which provide a mathematical basis for the discussion that follows. This chapter will briefly describe types of probability and nonprobability samples and their relative merits, and will also deal with sample size and the sampling fraction.

An introduction to probability sampling

In a probability sample, the chance each case had of being included can be estimated. This estimate can be made only if the sample has been created by random selection. *Random selection* means that each case in the population was given a chance of being in the sample, with sample cases selected by using such techniques as flips of the coin, rolls of dice, or a table of random numbers prepared especially for this purpose. Random selection allows us to calculate the probability that the result for the sample is similar to what exists in the population. In other words, from a probability sample we can determine the chance that the distributions of cases on variables in the sample represent the distributions in the population. This is extremely important because, as stated earlier, samples are studied to learn about populations. Nonprobability samples do not possess this important characteristic.

A total of 10 people live on a Caribbean Island. Their names are listed in Table 7.1 along with the number of clinic visits each made last year. The mean number of visits for the population is 4.5 (0 + 1 +2. . . + 9 ÷ 10 = 4.5). If all possible combinations of 4 distinct persons were made in which no two combinations contained the same 4 persons (for example, one combination would be John-Marsha-Tom-Dick, and another Marsha-Tom-Dick-Harry), there would be 210 combinations. If the mean number of clinic visits for each of 210 distinct 4-person combinations was calculated, the combinations would be distributed according to their means, as shown in Table 7.2. That is, two combinations would have mean

Table 7.1. Names of all island inhabitants and number of clinic visits made last year

Name	Number of visits
John	0
Marsha	1
Tom	2
Dick	3
Harry	4
Jane	5
Frieda	6
Ms. Jones	7
Lyle	8
Potjemann	9
Sum of visits	45
Number of inhabitants	10
Mean number of visits	4.5

scores under 2.00, 10 would have means which range from 2.00 to 2.67, and so forth.

In Table 7.2, more samples are in the same range as the population mean of 4.5 than are in any other range, and even more samples are included in the range of 2.75 to 5.67. The further from the population mean of 4.5, the fewer the combinations. If one were a betting person and had to wager even money on whether any one of the 210 combinations of 4 persons was closer to 4.5 or 2.0, the money should be placed on 4.5. It is this feature that allows us to calculate the chances that the sample is representative of a population. This is done in much the same spirit as the gambler who knows the odds and wins more than loses.

Suppose that the number of visits made by each islander last year is unknown; that is, the information in Table 7.1 is unavailable. For planning purposes we must estimate the number of visits made by the population, and to make that estimate we have only enough money to study four of the islanders. These four are

Table 7.2. Mean scores of distinct four-person combinations

Mean scores	Number of combinations
<2.00	2
2.00 − 2.67	10
2.75 − 3.25	25
3.33 − 4.00	43
4.17 − 4.83	50
5.00 − 5.67	43
5.75 − 6.25	25
6.33 − 7.00	10
>7.00	2

selected in a way that each has a known probability of being in the sample, that is, randomly. The number of visits each member of the sample made during the year is then obtained. Fortunately, statisticians have generated distributions like those in Table 7.2 so that it is unnecessary to know the actual population value of the variable of interest. A probability sample allows us to estimate the chance that the sample value for the variable is within a given range of the population value for that variable without knowing the latter. Suppose the numbers in Table 7.2 were generated by statisticians who knew nothing about the number of visits made by the study population. From these distributions, the probability that the mean number of clinic visits in the sample is within a given range of the population value can be calculated. The chances are 24 in 100 ($50/210 = .24$) that the sample value is within the range 4.17–4.83, and 60 in 100 ($43 + 50 + 43/210 = .60$) that it is within the range of 3.33–5.67. On the other hand, the chances are only 2 in 100 ($2 + 2/210 = .02$) that the population mean is less than 2.0 or more than 7.0. Thus, the chances that the mean of the sample is within various ranges of the population mean can be calculated, and the chances are in our favor that the sample estimate will be relatively close to the population mean. The important points are that these odds can be calculated when using probability samples and that information from the entire study population is not necessary for the calculations.

Types of probability samples

Three types of probability samples are commonly used: (1) simple random samples, (2) stratified random samples, and (3) cluster samples. For a *simple random sample* all cases in the population are listed, and sample cases are selected at random from that list so that each case has an equal chance of being in the sample. Say that the study population consists of 5,000 cases, and 500 cases are needed for the sample. Each of the 5,000 cases is assigned a number, the numbers are written on separate sheets of paper, the papers are folded so that the numbers cannot be seen, they are mixed thoroughly in a large fish bowl, and a blindfolded research assistant pulls 500 sheets from the bowl.

A *stratified random sample* is one in which simple random samples are selected within subcategories of a population. From a given population, for example, simple random samples of men and women are selected separately. The main reason for choosing this type of sampling plan is the suspicion that the subcategories, in this case the sexes, differ substantially on the variables of interest. If the association between sex and clinic utilization is being studied, and it is suspected that men and women differ significantly in utilization, it might be better to sample them separately. This could increase the chances that the sample distribution on the dependent variable would be nearer the population value than if sex was ignored by drawing a simple random sample from the entire population. If there is no reason to believe that important subgroups of the population differ substantially on the key variables of interest, then except for the condition noted in the following paragraph there is usually no reason for drawing a stratified random sample.

Stratified random samples can be either proportionate or disproportionate depending on whether the cases are drawn in proportion to their distribution in the population. Say that there are 1,000 men and 4,000 women in the population; that is, 20 percent of the population is male and 80 percent is female. If a sample of 500 is drawn in such a way that 20 percent are men and 80 percent are women (100 men and 400 women), it would be a proportionate stratified random sample. If, on the other hand, the sample is drawn so that half are men and half women, it would be a disproportionate sample. The purpose of disproportionate sampling usually is to make certain that there are enough cases for a particular analysis. For example, if there had been 200 men and 4,800 women in the population, and it was necessary to have at least 150 men in the sample, a proportionate sample of 500 men and women would yield only about 20 men since 4 percent of the population are men. Thus, the sample could be drawn disproportionately by randomly selecting 150 men and 350 women.

Sometimes it is extremely expensive to list all cases in the population for sampling purposes, or the cases are spread so thin geographically that it would be too expensive to obtain the necessary information from them. For example, if the study population is all people aged fifteen to forty-four living in U.S. cities with more than 250,000 residents, or all seventh graders in North Carolina public schools, it might be economically unfeasible to derive a list of all cases in these populations. If such a complete list could be obtained, it might still be too expensive to contact the widely spread sample cases. Instead, *cluster samples* could be used. The key feature of cluster sampling is that initially aggregates (clusters) rather than individual cases are selected randomly. This may be done in several stages. For example, all U.S. cities with a population over 250,000 might be listed, then 25 of the cities selected randomly, then census tracts in those cities listed and 50 tracts selected randomly; finally, people aged fifteen to forty-four living in these tracts would be selected randomly for study.

Nonprobability samples
Nonprobability samples do not use the random selection procedures of probability samples. Instead, cases are selected for convenience, usually a less expensive approach. Because random selection is not used, the chance a member of the population has

of being in the sample cannot be calculated; therefore, the probability that the sample reflects the population cannot be determined. This is, of course, a severe limitation when one is studying samples to learn about populations. Tests of statistical significance, important aids to analysis, are based on probability rather than nonprobability samples (see Chapter 10). Selection bias might produce misleading results, a problem that will be discussed later in this chapter.

Types of nonprobability samples

Basically, there are three types of nonprobability samples: (1) accidental, (2) quota, and (3) purposive. Suppose it is necessary to obtain information from a population of 5,000 by sampling 500 cases. In *accidental sampling* information is gathered from the 500 without using random selection to determine which of the 5,000 cases enter the sample. If a sample of 500 people aged fifteen to forty-four living in U.S. cities with a population over 250,000 is needed, it would be easy to go to a nearby city of that size and interview 500 people of the specified age. Those 500 might be selected because all of them shop at supermarkets on given days, all pass the same busy intersections during the day, or all happen to be at home in particular neighborhoods when the interviewers are working. With accidental samples it is impossible to estimate the chances that cases in the population had of being in the sample. Therefore, it is impossible to determine the probability that findings for the sample are similar to what exists in the population.

A *quota sample* is a type of accidental sample. Imagine again that a sample of 500 from a population of 5,000 is needed to estimate clinic utilization, and it is suspected that age is a related factor. That is, it is believed that people aged thirty to forty-four are more likely to use the clinic than those aged fifteen to twenty-nine. Suppose, further, that 25 percent of the population were in the older age group and 75 percent in the younger age group. If the sample contained more older than younger people—older people were easier to find at home, more likely to use the particular supermarket where our survey was being conducted, or for some other reason were more likely to enter the sample—then a higher clinic utilization rate would exist in the sample than in the population. Quota sampling attempts to correct for this by accidental sampling within age groups until the distribution by age in the sample equals that in the population. Thus, our data collectors would be instructed to gather information until they had reached 375 people aged fifteen to twenty-nine and 125 aged thirty to forty-four. The distribution by age in the sample would then equal the distribution in the population. However, although this corrects for the age distribution, the chances that distributions of other variables in the sample represent those in the population cannot be estimated because random selection procedures were not employed.

A *purposive sample* is one in which cases are selected because they supposedly represent the wider population. I might believe that one city is fairly representative of most in the United States, and within it interview people I judge representative of those aged fifteen to forty-four until my sample numbers 500 cases. Again, since there is no way to determine the chances that cases had of being in the sample, there is no definite way to assess the chances that the sample and population distributions are similar.

Selection bias

When human judgment rather than random selection is used to draw a sample—and this is the situation in all nonprobability samples—*selection bias* may distort the sample. Interviewers who arc simply told to contact cases until they have reached a certain number will probably choose the cases easiest to reach. If such cases are not representative of the population—which also contains cases more difficult to contact—the sample will be skewed by selection bias. Respondents who happen to be at home when the interviewer arrives are probably different from others in terms of such characteristics as age, employment, and marital status. Thus, the sample would differ from the population on such characteristics. If researchers studying the influence of caseload on family functioning choose families by nonrandom procedures, they may select those they think have the best chance of benefiting from the program, are unusually cooperative, or have convenient work schedules in terms of the research. Thus, the sample would contain bias due to selection, and this might influence the results of the study.

The subjects who agree to participate in research can also be the source of selection bias. If subjects are recruited through newspaper advertisement, not all persons in the population of interest will decide to respond. Those who do and those who do not could differ substantially, and the results would be influenced accordingly. Or, if 50 families are selected for the caseload study from a population of 1,000 merely by taking the first 50 who agree to participate, those 50 may differ from the remaining 950 on variables important to the study.

All nonprobability samples may have selection bias, and usually there is no way to determine whether the biases are influencing the findings. Probability samples remove human judgment from the selection process and are therefore much less likely to be influenced by selection bias.

Attrition

Selecting a sample randomly is not the same as ending up with a random sample. In addition, most of the sample cases must actually provide information throughout the life of the study. A perfectly selected random sample in which only 20 percent of the cases complete the study becomes a nonrandom sample. Moreover, under this condition bias can be substantial. The cases that do not complete a study may differ from those that do on variables of key importance to the study. Again, it may not be possible to adjust for these variables. Thus, researchers try to minimize the attrition that results from such factors as difficulty in locating cases, apathy of prospective participants, and the like. It is unrealistic to expect that 100 percent of a sample will actually participate throughout the study. But when the figure drops much below 70 percent, there is reason to be concerned about the effects this may have on the findings.

Sample size

Sometimes the findings of a study are discounted solely because the sample was small. Yet, when the sample is not extremely small—say 25 or more—and the cases were selected randomly, the results should not simply be dismissed. The reason, once again, is that when probability sampling is used, the chances that the sample will approximate the population can often be estimated. Such estimates take sample size into account, and sometimes they will suffice even when the sample is small.

Assume that a social welfare organization serves 1,000,000 families, and it is necessary to estimate how many of those families are poor. Lacking the funds to contact all the families, we draw a simple random sample of 100 from the population and find that 40 percent of these families are poor. Some persons might automatically conclude that the sample is too small to pay attention to this result. Because this is a probability sample, however, formulas can be used to estimate the chance that the percentage of poor people in the population lies within a specified range of the percentage of poor people in the sample of 100. The mathematics are beyond our scope here, but applying such formulas to our example would show that in 95 out of 100 samples from the population, 30 to 50 percent of the cases would be poor. This range is called the *confidence interval*. Stated somewhat differently, the chances are 95 out of 100 that 30 to 50 percent of the families in the population are poor. In 5 out of 100 samples the proportion of poor people would not be within the confidence interval of 30 to 50 percent. The point is that these chances and intervals can be calculated when probability samples are used, and the calculations take sample size into account.

For many purposes the precision of estimates based on confidence intervals is sufficient. Suppose, the number of poor families in the population must be known to prepare part of next year's budget for an agency activity that is estimated to cost $1 per poor family in the population. Suppose further that the activity is needed but not of highest priority, and those families that do not receive it will not be seriously affected. Moreover, it is necessary to keep the agency's total budget at a minimum. Extrapolating from the sample, the chances are 95 in 100 that there are 300,000 to 500,000 poor families in the population. Accordingly, $400,000 is budgeted for the activity. The chances are 5 in 100 that there is an error of more than 100,000 families, and that $100,000 has been either overbudgeted or underbudgeted. One would feel more comfortable with this decision based on a sample from a population of 1,000,000 than on educated guesswork alone.

Imagine, however, that the estimate had to be made because the agency's board had decided that new dwelling units were to be constructed for 5 percent of the poor families in the service area. Assuming one dwelling unit per family, and using the information from the sample of 100, the chances are 95 in 100 that 15,000 (300,000 families × 5 percent) to 25,000 (500,000 families × 5 percent) new units are needed. It might be decided to begin building 20,000 units. But if the poor actually make up 30 percent of the population, this represents an excess of 5,000 units. The board would not be pleased with this error; if each unit cost $45,000, it might represent an overspending of $225,000,000.

Clearly, the nature of the question to be addressed by the study, and the possible consequences of the answer, must be considered in determining the size of probability samples. It is true that the larger the sample, the narrower the confidence interval. This is illustrated in Table 7.3 (in which the values were created by standard procedures beyond the scope of this book). The left-hand column shows different percentages of the sample that could have the characteristic under study. The other columns show the confidence intervals for these percentages depending on different sample sizes. The bottom row indicates that a finding of 40 percent from a sample of 25 gives us odds of 95 in 100 that the population percentage falls within the interval 40 ± 19, or between 21 and 59 percent. If this finding came from a sample of 800 cases, the

Table 7.3. Confidence intervals for different percentages and sample sizes*

Sample percentage	Sample size					
	25	50	100	200	400	800
5	±8	±6	±4	±3	±2	±2
10	±12	±8	±6	±4	±3	±2
20	±16	±11	±8	±6	±4	±3
40	±19	±14	±10	±7	±5	±3

*Assumes a simple random sample, a large population, and being correct in 95 out of 100 samples.

chances are 95 in 100 that the population value falls within the interval 40 ± 3, that is, between 37 and 43 percent. In the case of a large and expensive construction program, it would obviously be worthwhile to use a sample of more than 25 or 100 cases. Note, however, that the difference in intervals between samples of 400 and 800 is small. The cost of obtaining information from 800 cases might not be justifiable given the difference in two percentage points between intervals; however, this depends on the nature of the question being addressed and the consequences to be expected from the decision. As a rule, one needs to increase the chances of being correct, and hence to have larger samples, to the degree that harm or excess cost could result from an estimate that is much different from the actual population value.

In all the above calculations and examples, the chance of being correct in 95 of 100 samples was acceptable. That is a common level of confidence but is chosen rather arbitrarily. For some problems it might be necessary to increase or decrease the chances of being correct, say to be 99 times in 100 or 85 times in 100. Again, such considerations as cost, potential harm, and importance of the results influence choice of the most appropriate confidence level.

The sampling fraction

The *sampling fraction* is the number of cases in the sample divided by the number of cases in the population. One often hears that when the sampling fraction is very small—that is, when the sample is a small portion of the population from which it was drawn—the findings for the sample are unlikely to represent the population. Actually, when the population is large (and if this were not usually the case, we would not bother with sampling), the sampling fraction makes a small contribution to the confidence interval. This is illustrated in Table 7.4. The number of sample cases remains a constant 100 in this table, and the percentage of sample members with the characteristic under study also remains constant at 40 percent. Instead, the population size varies; hence the sampling fraction, and the confidence intervals for these different fractions, are presented. Note that the confidence interval changes from 8.9 to 9.9 when the sampling fraction declines from .20 to .0001, and only 9.5 to 9.9 when the fraction goes from .10 to .0001. The sampling fraction is not nearly as influential on confidence intervals as sample size, and since the total populations are usually large, it ordinarily makes a negligible contribution to the confidence interval.

Sampling and other ingredients of research

An adequately developed hypothesis usually indicates the population to be studied. To test the hypotheses used in the preceding chapters, samples were drawn from large U.S. cities (to determine if fertility changed in response to a mass media campaign), enrollees of a prepaid medical program (to study the relationship between stress and use of the program), and American children aged one to four (to show their immunization status).

The principles of sampling are directly applicable to the intervention and nonintervention designs used in causal research. To study the hypothesis that a reduction in caseload for caseworkers enhances family functioning, a probability or nonprobability sample of all families eligible for the service could be selected. To

Table 7.4. Confidence intervals for different sampling fractions when the sample contains 100 cases and 40 percent of the sample possesses the characteristic*

Population size	Sampling fraction	Confidence interval for 40 percent
500	.2000	±8.9
1,000	.1000	±9.5
2,000	.0500	±9.7
4,000	.0250	±9.8
8,000	.0120	±9.9
16,000	.0060	±9.9
1,000,000	.0001	±9.9

*Assumes a simple random sample and being correct in 95 of 100 samples.

test the hypothesis that psychological stress increases visits to a prepaid group medical practice, a sample of cases from all participants in that program might be chosen for study.

Moreover, units of study other than families or individuals can be sampled. Samples from all U.S. cities might be drawn to study the influence of a mass media campaign upon fertility, or from 100 clinics to examine the relationship between distance to the clinic and clinic utilization. Again, the same principles of probability and nonprobability sampling presented above apply when these different units are sampled.

Sampling is also important to the research methods discussed in the following chapters. Chapter 9 presents the basic features of contingency table analysis. The application of this method can be influenced by the sampling plan used. Indeed, the sampling plan is often determined in part by whether contingency table analysis is to be applied. Sampling is also important in using the tests of statistical significance discussed in Chapter 10; these important tools are based on the principles of probability sampling.

References

Cochran, William G. (1977) *Sampling Techniques.* New York: John Wiley and Sons.

Kish, Leslie (1965) *Survey Sampling.* New York: John Wiley and Sons.

Stuart, Alan (1968) *Basic Ideas of Scientific Sampling.* London: Charles Griffin Company, Ltd.

8

Measurement

Measurement is the assignment of values of variables to cases. When individuals have been assigned dollar values to represent their incomes, the variable "income" has been measured. Sex is measured when some people are classified as male and others as female. Similarly, immunization status, psychological stress, and the economic level of cities are measured when cases are assigned to categories of these variables. Measurement is an essential ingredient of all research.

Measurement is usually much more complex than these examples indicate. Indeed, even apparently simple variables can become complicated measurement problems. Is it more relevant to measure individual or family income, and should this include dollars before or after taxes, money earned from a lottery, and products received in lieu of direct payment for service? There are obvious ways to categorize people according to sex, but if this depends on classifying photographs of young people taken in the 1970s, styles of hair and dress could lead to confusion.

Adequate hypotheses identify many of the variables to be measured in a study. The hypothesis that maternal-infant attachment will be facilitated by early and extended contact indicates that we must measure at least two variables: maternal-infant attachment and early and extended contact. Similarly, the hypothesis that the use of drugs by peers influences the use of drugs by others requires that we measure at least peer and subject use of drugs. Hypotheses often suggest other variables which need to be measured. To test hypotheses adequately, we may need to identify intervening variables or determine if the associations are spurious. Thus, we must measure many variables in addition to those considered to be independent and dependent.

The myth that "some variables can't be measured"

It is often said that some variables cannot be measured. Among these are mother-infant attachment, most feelings including love, and psychological stress. If this were true, then many important questions in community health and welfare could not be studied. Fortunately, all variables may be considered measurable when it is recognized that measurement is a process by which people define and describe. That is, variables exist as a result of their definitions and descriptions. A researcher might define attachment of a mother to her infant as close and affectionate behavior toward the baby. Some mothers kiss and cuddle their babies, whereas others leave them alone in the cradle. The variable "attachment" is measured by categorizing mothers according to how much they kiss and cuddle their babies. Or one could define the "pregnancy wantedness" of husbands in terms of their psychological reactions to their wives' pregnancies and ask a group of husbands if they are happy or sad, embarrassed or proud. The variable "pregnancy wantedness" would then be defined by categorizing the fathers according to their statements. Some people might not agree with the way attachment and pregnancy wantedness were defined and described, and some researchers might require the use of more systematic procedures and more elaborate definitions and descriptions. Nonetheless, the definitions and descriptions in these examples are acts of measurement, even though some might be considered crude. Lundberg (1964) offers a more detailed discussion of the measurability of variables.

To declare all variables measurable is not to say that they are measured with comparable ease and accuracy. Indeed, measurement problems range substantially among variables in community health and welfare. One major source of such differences is whether we have explicit and agreed-upon criteria for measurement. The criteria for measuring birth weight, height, and body temperature are well established. A scale, ruler, or thermometer will be used, and although the measurements will not be completely accurate, if they are done carefully the error will be minimal. There is less consensus on the criteria for classifying new babies according to the normalcy of birth weight, people as short or tall, and the body temperature that requires hospitalization. A group of experts would not agree completely on how to classify cases across categories of these variables. There would probably be even less consensus on the criteria for measuring such variables as maternal-infant attachment, psychological stress, and drug abuse.

Measurement error and its sources

Measurement error occurs when cases are assigned to the wrong categories of variables. If a person earns an annual salary of $5,000 but is assigned to a $10,000 category, this is an error of measurement. Measurement error is impossible to eliminate because it has many sources; we can never be certain that we have been completely successful in controlling it. The goal, instead, is to minimize measurement error so that it does not invalidate the conclusions drawn from a study. We attempt to do so by careful definition of variables, selection of items which best represent the definitions, and repeated examination of these items, especially in pilot studies, until assured that the domain has been covered adequately.

The criteria chosen to measure a variable can be an important source of measurement error. Suppose we have defined heroin abuse as "negative effects for self or others from using heroin." Subjects must be classified according to whether they abuse heroin, and to do this we might ask them three questions:

1. Have you ever hurt yourself by taking heroin?
2. Have you ever harmed a friend when taking heroin?
3. Have you ever caused an accident when using heroin?

A positive response to any of these questions classifies a subject as a heroin abuser. But these three questions may not be sufficient according to our definition of heroin abuse. We may also need to know whether job performance has been harmed by heroin use, whether people other than a friend have been harmed when heroin was used, and whether crimes were committed as a consequence of heroin use.

Words and phrases can be ambiguous and are therefore sources of measurement error. What precisely is meant by "hurt yourself," "harmed," and "accident?" Some might consider pain from a needle as "hurt," whereas others might believe that an injury requiring hospitalization is necessary for this label. To some, harming another person might mean physical punishment, whereas for others it might include verbal assault. It is easy to see how such ambiguities could lead to measurement error. The language used to describe variables must be carefully examined, and meanings must be clarified for subjects, interviewers, and observers. There is no substitute for trying out questions, observation categories, and definitions in pilot studies before deriving final measures that are sufficiently explicit.

Another important source of measurement error consists of questions which might be embarrassing to answer, or which may lead to a socially desirable but not necessarily truthful response. It is illegal to use heroin, and a subject might falsify responses for protection. Clearly, it is not socially desirable to admit to heroin use except perhaps when one is among heroin users. Some racially prejudiced people might report that they are not prejudiced if they believe that response is socially preferred. One major mechanism for reducing this source of error is to assure anonymity and confidentiality of data to the subjects.

Other sources of measurement error are personal and situational. A person being interviewed might be tired and for this reason give incorrect responses. The husband's presence while his wife is being interviewed about her behavior with drugs could produce distorted responses, as might the distractions of children and television. Observations of interaction between mother and infant at the end of a busy day might not yield measures typical of a mother's behavior. To minimize these sources of measurement error, one can conduct interviews privately, in quiet settings, and when subjects are not tired. Questions requiring concentration may be asked early in an interview rather than later when attention might be decreased, and the data collection methods may be scrutinized in pilot studies to minimize the time involved.

The researchers themselves can produce measurement error. Observers do not always follow instructions carefully. They may invent their own explanation of the study, ask parents to be present during observation when the plan calls for their absence, or otherwise depart from a study's protocol in ways that produce error. An interviewer who changes the wording of questions or the order in which they are asked could also produce measurement error. A woman interviewing a man about his sexual behavior might elicit inaccurate responses. Proper selection and training of observers and interviewers, with close supervision of their work, are prerequisites for controlling many sources of measurement error related to administration.

Another source of measurement error is recording and processing. Observers and interviewers can mark the wrong boxes on forms. Persons responsible for preparing data for analysis sometimes transfer information incorrectly. Those who punch the information on cards for computer processing sometimes strike the wrong key. And finally, computer programers have been known to make errors that yield incorrect classification of cases.

These, then, are some of the major sources of measurement error. Clearly, there is no substitute for carefully piloted instruments and procedures, proper selection and training of personnel, and rigorous surveillance of the entire research process, including that important portion which pertains to measurement. Again, the objective of these activities is to reduce measurement error so that it has minimal influence on the results of research.

Measures are traditionally and meaningfully considered in terms of their reliability and validity. *Reliability* refers to the extent to which items are related to one another in expected ways, or to the stability of the measure upon repeated application. *Validity,* on the other hand, is the degree to which a measure reflects what was intended to be measured.

Reliability

A measure must have an acceptable level of reliability in order to be useful in research. To be considered reliable, a measure must classify cases with acceptable consistency and stability. If we classify a person as a drug abuser on Tuesday and a nonabuser on Wednesday, and the drug behavior of that person has not changed, then for that case our classification is inconsistent. Thus, we do not know if that person should be considered an abuser or a nonabuser of drugs for the study. If many cases are classified inconsistently, then the measure is too unreliable for use in research.

Suppose that in another study attachment has been defined as close and affectionate maternal behavior toward the baby. Two colleagues watch mothers as they interact with their infants, observing the same mother at the same time and marking a check sheet which describes her behavior. For example. each observer indicates whether the mother kissed and hugged the baby during the period of observation. If one observer using this process classifies the mother as attached and another observer classifies her as unattached, then for that mother the classification is inconsistent.

Another type of inconsistency involves the items used to measure the variable. We might use hugging and kissing to measure attachment on the grounds that mothers with positive attachment should hug and kiss their babies more often than mothers with less positive attachment. However, if mothers who hug their babies kiss their babies less often than mothers who rarely hug their babies, then we have an inconsistency in measurement: If both hugging and kissing are positive indicators of attachment, then they should be related in a consistent direction.

Many of the examples above identify influences which can lower the reliability of measures, and some of the procedures used to increase reliability were mentioned. If a person responding to questions related to drug abuse behavior does not understand some of the vocabulary or is uncertain that the data will be handled confidentially, this might produce measurement error. To reduce this source of error, we would make certain that the vast majority of our subjects understand the words used, that they are not too tired when answering our questions, and that they understand and believe our procedures for assuring confidentiality.

Various methods are used to determine the reliability of measures. Several of the more commonly used techniques are summarized below. Except for interobserver reliability, these techniques are categorized according to whether they assess stability or equivalence. The central question regarding stability is: how reliable are the measures upon repeated application? Methods assessing equivalence are typically used when measurements have been made at one point in time, and the focus is upon the interrelationships among items which comprise the measure.

Stability

When attempting to determine reliability by the *test-retest* method, the same measure is used at least two different times for the same cases. For example, suppose we have a series of questions designed to measure drug abuse behavior. If we administer them to the same subjects on two occasions two weeks apart and have no reason to believe that their behavior with drugs changed during that period, then the greater the consistency of their drug behavior for both administrations, the more confidence we may have in the reliability of the measure. Or we might observe and record the interaction of twenty-five mothers and their infants at 1 P.M. on Monday and Wednesday, rating their behavior toward their babies in categories believed to reflect attachment. If most of the cases receive similar scores both times, then the measure is assumed to have acceptable reliability. If many cases are classified differently at the times of test and retest, and there is no reason to believe that their attachment behavior changed, then the measure is considered relatively unreliable.

This procedure for assessing reliability has two problems. First, there is always the chance that change did occur between measurement points. Perhaps some of the drug abusers stopped abusing drugs, or mothers became more attached to their babies between the times of measurement. The distribution of cases on the measure should then differ. If the change in behavior goes undetected, a weak association between the variables could be erroneously attributed to unreliable measurement.

A second problem with the test-retest method is that if the measurement points are too close together, the subject might remember the earlier answers and respond accordingly. This can produce high associations and a misleading suggestion of reliability. Or the observers of mothers and children might remember their earlier observations and rate the mothers accordingly, again producing strong associations and an inflated indication of reliability.

The *parallel forms* procedure is meant to correct for the test-retest problem of earlier measures influencing later measures through recall. In this procedure, two different instruments are devised to measure the same thing. For example, 50 different questions might be drawn up to measure drug abuse behavior and then randomly assigned to Set A and Set B. Set A is administered to the subjects on the first occasion and Set B to the same subjects later. The degree to which persons are classified similarly with Sets A and B is an indication of the reliability of our measure, assuming no behavior change. Or we might identify 100 behaviors thought to indicate mother-infant attachment and randomly allocate 50 to Set A and 50 to Set B. An observer completes Set A on Monday and Set B on Wednesday. Since the observer is marking different behaviors on both days, the marks given on Wednesday do not reflect the memory of the marks given on Monday. The degree of association between A and B is an indication of the reliability of the measure of attachment.

Equivalence

In measuring many variables, different items are used and then combined to represent the variables. For example, 50 questions might be asked to classify people according to their abuse of drugs, and to measure attachment many behaviors might be observed in addition to hugging and kissing. When using multiple items, we reason that each item is actually one indicator of the more general variable of interest and that the composite of items is a better measure of the variable than any single one. If each item is an indicator of the more general variable, then there should be *equivalence*—consistent patterns of relationships among the various items. Mothers who hug their babies should also be more likely to kiss them than mothers who do not hug their babies if both behaviors reflect the variable of attachment. People who hurt themselves by using heroin should also be more likely to hurt others as a result than heroin users who do not hurt themselves. Thus, the degree to which items are interrelated reflects the consistency or reliability of a measure.

The *split-half technique* for assessing reliability follows this reasoning. Items are administered to the same subjects once, and through random allocation the items are then split into two groups. The items for the groups are then summed in such a way that each case has two scores for the variable. Thus, a subject would have two measures of drug abuse behavior, each based on 25 separate items. The stronger the relationship between these two measures, the greater the equivalence of items and hence the higher the reliability of the measure.

Another approach to assessing reliability, sometimes referred to as *internal consistency,* relies upon the same basic idea as split-half reliability: Since multiple items are being used to measure a common variable, then the individual items should be consistently related to one another. However, rather than splitting the items into two groups and then determining their equivalence, the items are analyzed by direct manipulation of all of them. A number of statistical procedures have been developed to assess reliability in this way (Summers, 1970).

Interobserver reliability

A common method of assessing reliability when using observers to collect data is to have two or more observers measure the same subjects at the same time. For example, two observers may rate maternal-infant attachment during the same observation period. If there is a strong association between their ratings, then the measure is considered reliable. If the association is weak, then the measure is judged to be unreliable.

Validity

Validity is central to measurement. A measure is valid if it actually measures what was meant to be measured. The number of days absent from school has been used as an indicator of child health status, but this measure might be of unacceptable validity if many children are absent for reasons other than poor health. Medical examinations might prove to be a more valid measure of health status. Attitudes toward premarital sexual permissiveness have been used as indicators of sexual behavior, but they may be imperfect measures of actual sexual experience.

Researchers rely on four main methods of determining validity. These methods can be applied to measures of most variables relevant to community health and welfare.

Face validity

A measure is said to have "face validity" when it is considered to be valid "on the face of it." That is, the validity of the measure depends on a personal judgment of how well it appears to reflect what was intended to be measured. One compares the measure with the definition of the variable to be measured and makes a decision about the validity of the measure.

Although face validation is used frequently, being clearly the least expensive and simplest procedure to apply, it is too dependent upon the individual to be considered definitive. This is not to say that it plays no role in research. When measures are first being developed, their assessment for face validity must play some role. Before using the more rigorous validation techniques discussed below, researchers usually make an informal comparison between the definition and the proposed measure of a variable. And when examining the quality of measures used in other research, face validation is often used if the studies did not incorporate more systematic validation techniques.

Content validity

A measure is said to have *content validity* when the items used are representative of the universe of things believed to indicate the variable. When the universe is not represented by the measure, then it is considered to lack content validity. *Content validation* is the process of determining the degree to which the domain of the variable is reflected by the measure.

Attachment, like all other variables, can be reflected by many different indicators. In addition to kissing and cuddling, one might include the frequency with which an infant is soothed, rocked, played with, smiled at, talked to, hugged, and cared for with respect to health needs. The more representative our measure is of all behaviors that reflect attachment, the more confidence we have in the content validity of our measure of attachment.

Creating a measure with content validity demands much more systematic and detailed consideration than is required for face validity. The researcher must attempt to identify the universe of indicators believed to reflect the measure of concern, and then to select a random sample of the indicators to make certain that the universe is represented by the measure. This is, of course, an ideal; in practice, the entire universe of indicators can never be identified. Nonetheless, it is an ideal toward which the researcher can strive, and this is not a requirement for face validation. Moreover, content validation typically requires the researcher to review the literature, perform a pilot study, and obtain expert assistance in establishing the universe of indicators. For example, we might review earlier research to identify all behaviors others believed to indicate attachment, interview mothers to learn what behaviors they believe are important, and draw up a similar list from persons with expertise in mother-infant relationships. Then we would sample randomly from this composite and use the sample as our measure.

Content validation, like face validation, depends on some subjective judgments by the researcher. And content validation does not necessarily correct the many sources of error inherent in face validation. We might have a representative set of behaviors thought to reflect attachment but still be measuring something else. It is, however, a more rigorous and systematic, and less subjective approach.

Criterion-related validity

To test a measure by the method of criterion-related validation requires at least two things: (1) the measure to be validated (index measure) and (2) a different measure believed to measure the same variable more directly (criterion measure). The association between the index and criterion measures is taken as an indication of criterion-related validity. Index measures are often used rather than criterion measures in research, usually because the former are relatively inexpensive to implement.

Imagine that we have developed the questions shown in table 8.1 to be used in interviewing mothers for the purpose of measuring attachment. They comprise our index measure of attachment. Before administering these questions to a sample of 1,000 mothers, we would like some assurance that the measure is of acceptable validity. We have experienced social workers conduct in-depth couseling sessions with 100 mothers comparable to those who will be in our study. Using the results of these sessions, the social workers determine how close and affectionate the mothers seem to be toward their infants. This rating is our criterion measure of attachment. We apply our index measure to the same 100 mothers, obtaining their answers to the same questions. The more

Table 8.1. Items used to measure mother-infant attachment

During the last seven days, how often have you:	Often	Sometimes	Seldom	Never
kissed your baby	4	3	2	1
cuddled your baby	4	3	2	1
soothed your baby	4	3	2	1
rocked your baby	4	3	2	1
played with your baby	4	3	2	1
smiled at your baby	4	3	2	1
talked to your baby	4	3	2	1
hugged your baby	4	3	2	1

strongly related the index and criterion measures, the more valid our index measure. If the interview and criterion measures are weakly associated, related in opposite directions (high attachment on one measure indicates low attachment on the other), or not related at all, the validity of the index measure is questionable.

Counseling sessions with social workers is not the only way to assess the criterion-related validity of our index measure of attachment. We could have observers independently rate the mothers according to how close and affectionate their behavior is while they are bathing the babies. The observers could indicate how often the mother kissed the baby, whether she handled the baby gently or roughly, and whether or not she talked with the baby during bathing. These observations would serve as the criterion measure of attachment. We could then ask the 100 mothers to answer the index measure questions in an interview. The degree to which the index and criterion measures of attachment are related indicates the criterion-related validity of the index measure.

In the application of criterion-related validity methods, one does not expect perfect relationships between index and criterion measures. Moderate to strong relationships are sufficient.

Criterion validation is a relatively well accepted method for assessing the validity of a measure. One limitation of this method is that when no criterion is available, it cannot be used. Moreover, a modest or nonexistent relationship between the measure of interest and the criterion might be due to measurement error in the criterion. Thus, even when there is a low or moderate relationship between index and criterion measures, the index measure might be valid and the criterion measure invalid.

Construct validity

In *construct validation*, hypotheses are formulated about the relationships between the variable represented by the index measure and measures of noncriterion variables presumed to have acceptable validity. These hypotheses are then tested by research. In other words, we place the variable represented by the index measure within a theory, derive hypotheses from the theory, and then test the hypotheses. To the extent that the hypotheses are confirmed, we have confidence in the construct validity of the index measure.

Imagine that we plan to administer the questions shown in Table 8.1 to 1,000 mothers when their infants are four months old. However, before doing so, we want some assurance that these items are an acceptably valid measure of attachment. We reason that if the measure is valid, then it should be related to other variables in expected ways, as suggested by a theory that incorporates the index measure. Thus, we hypothesize that mothers fifteen to nineteen years of age are less attached to their infants than mothers twenty to twenty-four years of age because younger mothers are less mature psychologically than older mothers. We also hypothesize that mothers who did not want to become pregnant are less attached to their four-month-old infants than mothers who wanted the pregnancy. Finally, we hypothesize, on the basis of prior research and theory, that mothers who are physically close to their babies during extended periods after delivery become more attached to them than mothers who are separated from their infants during that period. We do a series of studies to test these hypotheses, using measures of the variables—age of mother, psychological maturity, pregnancy wantedness, physical closeness after delivery—which have been demonstrated by earlier research to have acceptable validity. If the findings prove consistent with the theory, the index measure is assumed to have construct validity. Testing of additional hypotheses could give this assumption further support.

Construct validation is usually the most expensive and time-consuming method of assessing validity, and it depends upon valid measures of other variables. Moreover, this method requires a well-formulated theoretical framework and prior research. When hypotheses are rejected by construct validation studies, we are never absolutely certain whether this indicates that the index measure is invalid, the measures of the other variables are invalid, or the theory incorporating the variable of interest is faulty. With the accumulation of research findings, however, we can judge how much confidence to have in the validity of a measure. Construct validation is considered by many researchers to be the most convincing of validation procedures, expecially when there are no adequate measures available for criterion validation.

On validity and reliability

A measure could be extremely reliable and completely invalid. A measure of maternal attachment could produce similar results with separate but comparable measures over time and with substantial agreement among observers, but still not be an acceptably valid measure of attachment. A mother unattached to her child might consistently exhibit behavior which suggests to observers that she is attached. Drug abusers might consistently report that they have never abused a drug when in fact they have. These measures would be reliable but invalid. A measure must be sufficiently reliable to achieve acceptable validity, but a reliable measure might be invalid.

Multiple-item scales

Researchers have developed a variety of procedures to combine information in such a way that single scores to represent a variable can be assigned to cases. These are called *multiple-item scales*. The questions in Table 8.1 are elements of such a scale. During an interview, mothers respond to the questions by circling a number from 1 to 4 next to each behavior, and the scale is formed by summing these numbers. Thus, each mother is assigned a single score for the measure of attachment, ranging from 32 (often exhibited each behavior) to 8 (never exhibited any of the behaviors). The higher the score, the more attached we consider the mother. This type of multi-item scale is appropriately called a *summated scale*.

There are three major reasons for using scales. The first is that they simplify data analyses. If we wished to determine whether there is an association between extended contact in the hospital and maternal attachment without forming a multi-item scale, then we would have to examine the possibility of association eight times, that is, separately for each item of the measure. When we calculate the sum of the items, there is one association to explore rather than eight. The gain in simplifying the analysis is much greater for measures that contain many more items than eight—for example, most of those for IQ, personality, attitude, and efficiency. Scales can substantially reduce the complexity of data for analysis.

A second reason for forming multiple-item scales is that we are typically attempting to measure a variable encompassing many items. When asking mothers how frequently they hug, kiss, and cuddle their babies, we are more interested in determining how attached they are toward their babies than how they behave on any item that indicates a single behavior. Thus, a composite of these items rather than a series of individual analyses places the data in a context more compatible with what we want to measure.

The third main reason for forming scales is that they generally increase reliability. That is, a combination of items yields more reliable measurement than single items within a scale; therefore, we can often reduce measurement error by use of scales.

Researchers have developed many different forms of multiple-item scales. Along with the summated scale, another commonly used type is *equal-appearing intervals.*

An equal-appearing interval scale differs substantially from a summated scale with respect to the way single scores are assigned to cases. Imagine that we have identified 100 behaviors thought to indicate attachment behavior, comparable to those in Table 8.1. We then have fifty experts on mother-infant relationships independently classify the items, assigning each to one of eleven categories based on their judgment of how much each reflects close and affectionate behavior. For example, one expert who considers kissing more close and affectionate behavior than talking to the baby might assign an 11 to kissing and a 2 to talking. Each expert does this for each item. When experts disagree on the categories to which items should be assigned, those items are discarded. Then, the median score for each item is calculated and the items are arrayed from a high median score ("high attachment") to a low median score ("relatively low attachment"). The final items selected are those which spread evenly across the 1 to 11 continuum. Mothers would then be asked to indicate which of these they had done during a specified period. For each behavior chosen, the median score derived through the judging process would be added, and the total would represent the subject's degree of attachment.

One advantage of this method of multiple-item scaling is that it is intended to generate differences between scores at any place on the entire continuum of scores which are equal to the differences at any other place on the continuum. For example, the difference between a score of 1 and 3 is meant to be equivalent to the difference between a score of 5 and 7, a claim that summation and most other multiple-item scaling procedures cannot make. This property makes scales developed through the technique of equal-appearing intervals more compatible with the assumptions of the relatively sophisticated statistical methods discussed in Chapter 10. The key disadvantage of the equal-appearing interval technique is its costliness compared to many other approaches.

On the fineness of measures

The *fineness* or precision of measures deserves special mention because misleading conclusions can be drawn from research if measurement is too crude. Imagine that we have identified 100 women with a history of neglect of their children, and that we want to find out if a program for facilitating mother-infant attachment will increase their attachment. We obtain measures of attachment by observing the mothers and their infants before the program and then allocate them randomly either to receive or not receive the program, thus producing groups which are similar on attachment before the program. We repeat our measure of attachment six months after the program. If our measure of attachment included only the two broad categories of "attached" and "unattached," as in the first column of Table 8.2, and the cases were distributed on that measure as shown in Table 8.2, then we would conclude that the program had no influence upon attachment since there are equal numbers of mothers in the two groups. Indeed, all these subjects remain unattached. But suppose we had used a finer measure of attachment, as in the second column of Table 8.2. Although none of the mothers shifted to the attached category, there was a substantial change in the experimental group relative to the control group, in the direction of a positive program effect. In this case, we would conclude that the program did increase mother-infant attachment.

Data collection methods

There are many different ways to collect data. Among the more common procedures are interviews, self-administered questionnaires, observation, and the use of existing records. Sometimes it is obvious which method should be used. If many of the research subjects are illiterate, then an interview rather than a self-administered questionnaire will be necessary. If a hypothesis suggests the need to measure an attitude, then subjects will probably be questioned rather than observed. Other factors in regard to data collection methods are less self-evident. A common factor is the

Table 8.2. Group membership and two measures of attachment (hypothetical data)

Measures of attachment:		Number of persons in:	
1	2	Experimental group	Control group
Attached	Extreme	0	0
	Moderate	0	0
	Slight	0	0
Unattached	Slight	48	2
	Moderate	2	5
	Extreme	0	43
	Total	50	50

amount of money available for that part of the research process. Having an observer rate the behavior of mothers in their homes might be more expensive than having the mothers respond to the questions of an interviewer, and having subjects complete a self-administered questionnaire in a group is usually less expensive than having an interviewer contact each subject at home.

A consideration of measurement error is often an important factor in choosing among data collection techniques. If the variables are particularly sensitive—such as drug abuse or premarital sexual behavior—then more honest responses and hence less measurement error may be obtained by self-administered questionnaires than by interviews, as the former is less personal and more assuring regarding anonymity and confidentiality. If observations might influence the behavior of interest—mothers might behave differently toward their infants when being viewed by observers than when the observers are not present—then interviews could be preferable.

More detailed sources
Excellent introductions to the strengths and weaknesses of various data collection methods can be found in Selltiz, Wrightsman, and Cook (1976). Cronbach (1971) is recommended for a clear

discussion of validity and Summers (1970) for a more comprehensive treatment of validity and many other facets of measurement. Although Cronbach places his discussion in the context of educational testing and Summers focuses upon the measurement of attitudes, the principles considered by both can be applied to many types of variables apart from those common to education and attitude research.

References

Cronbach, Lee J. (1971) "Test Validation." In *Educational Measurement,* edited by Robert Thorndike. 2nd ed. Washington, D.C.: American Council on Education. Pp. 443–507.

Lundberg, George A (1964) *Foundations of Sociology.* New York: David McKay. Pp. 51–97.

Selltiz, Claire; Wrightsman, Lawrence S.; and Cook, Stuart W., eds. (1976) *Research Methods in Social Relations.* New York: Holt, Rinehart and Winston.

Summers, Gene F. (1970) *Attitude Measurement.* Chicago: Rand McNally.

9
Contingency Table Analysis

As emphasized earlier, the identification of associations is an important research objective. *Contingency table analysis,* which generally involves distributing cases across categories of two or more variables simultaneously, is often used to analyze data in ways that hypotheses about associations can be accepted or rejected.

To illustrate contingency table analysis, hypothetical data will be used to test the hypothesis that women with few years of formal education are more likely to have one or more children than women with more years of formal education. After the basic principles of contingency table analysis are discussed in this context, further analyses will be presented from a study of the relationship between smoking behavior during pregnancy and birth weight.

The two-variable table
The first step in contingency table analysis is to cross-classify the independent variable (education in our example) and the dependent variable (number of children) so that each case enters the appropriate cell of the contingency table, as in Table 9.1.

Table 9.1. The relationship between education and number of children (hypothetical data)

Number of children	Years of education		
	<12	12	>12
1 or more	190	837	352
None	10	63	48
Total number	200	900	400

Of the 1,500 women in our hypothetical sample, 190 had fewer than 12 years of education and one or more children, and 352 had more than 12 years of education and one or more children.

Our hypothesis indicates that we must compare women with different levels of education with respect to their relative likelihood of having one or more children. Before making that comparison, we must take into account the fact that the number of women varies by educational category; that is, one category has 200 women, another has 900, and the third has 400. Thus, there will almost certainly be more women with one or more children in the group of 900 women who have had 12 years of education than in any other educational group simply because it is the largest group; there will also be more women with no children in this group for the same reason. It is clear that we must standardize across educational categories to take into account the different numbers of women in each category. One way to do this is to convert the number of cases to percentages.

The distributions in Table 9.1 have been converted to percentages in Table 9.2; they were calculated so that the total number of cases for each independent variable column would be 100 percent. In contingency table analysis, the rule of thumb for percentages is that the direction of calculation should be vertical, within columns of the independent variable, so that percentages can be compared across categories. Reading Table 9.2 horizontally, we see that the percentages with one or more children decrease as years of education increase; 95 percent of women with fewer than 12 years of education have one or more children, 93 percent with

Table 9.2. The relationship between education and number of children (hypothetical data)

Number of children	Years	of	education
	<12	12	>12
1 or more	95%	93%	88%
None	5	7	12
Total number	200	900	400
%	100	100	100

12 years of education have one or more children, and 88 percent with more than 12 years of education have one or more children. From this we conclude that (1) the independent and dependent variables are associated (as the percentages are read horizontally they are different, and therefore the two variables vary with one another) and (2) those with few years of formal education are more likely to have one or more children than those with relatively many years of formal education. These findings suggest that we should accept the hypothesis.

Imagine that the cases were distributed as they are in Table 9.3 rather than in Tables 9.1 and 9.2. We would then conclude that no association exists between education (independent variable) and number of children (dependent variable) because the percentages do not differ across columns of the independent variable.

A third situation is illustrated in Table 9.4, where the percentage of women with one or more children increases with the number of years of formal education—the opposite of what we would predict from our hypothesis.

Analyses with more than two variables
With findings like those shown in Tables 9.1 to 9.4, researchers usually continue the analysis at this stage since the introduction of more variables could alter the inference. They usually want to determine whether other variables are producing a spurious association between the independent and dependent variables, or

Table 9.3. The relationship between education and number of children (hypothetical data)

Number of children	Years of education		
	<12	12	>12
1 or more	94%	94%	94%
None	6	6	6
Total number	200	900	400
%	100	100	100

Table 9.4. The relationship between education and number of children (hypothetical data)

Number of children	Years of education		
	<12	12	>12
1 or more	88%	93%	95%
None	12	7	5
Total number	200	900	400
%	100	100	100

whether a third intervening variable explains a causal connection between them.

Age might be one of many variables that produces a spurious association between education and whether women have one or more children. Older women have had more time than younger women to accumulate years of formal education and to have children. If age explains the association between education and whether women have one or more children, this would negate the idea that the association is causal. That is, education and number of children would be associated because of their common relationship to age, and not because education determines the number of children.

When contingency analysis is used to identify variables that might produce spurious associations, cases are distributed by the independent and dependent variables within each category of the third variable that is suspected of producing a spurious relationship. When this is done, researchers often say that they are "controlling" for the third variable. Table 9.5 illustrates this procedure by controlling for the age of the women. The women were first separated according to three age groups. Contingency tables showing how education and number of children are related were then prepared for each group. Thus, Table 9.5 contains the format of three of any of our tables presented above. The conclusion depends upon the relationships within the subtables.

Table 9.5. The relationship between education and number of children, by age of mother (hypothetical data)

Number of children	Age 15–19 Years of education			Age 20–24 Years of education			Age 25–29 Years of education		
	<12	12	>12	<12	12	>12	<12	12	>12
1 or more	82%	90%	96%	87%	94%	97%	90%	96%	99%
None	18	10	4	13	6	3	10	4	1
Total number	67	300	133	67	300	133	66	300	134
%	100	100	100	100	100	100	100	100	100

If there are associations between the independent and dependent variables within each category of the control variable, then we conclude that this third variable does not account for the association. That is the conclusion drawn from table 9.5: An association between education and number of children is maintained regardless of age. The next step would be to conduct similar analyses with other variables to see if they produce a spurious association between the independent and dependent variables.

If we had originally found the association recorded in Table 9.4, controlled for age, and found that there were no associations between independent and dependent variables within age categories, then we would conclude that age accounts for the relationship between education and number of children. This is what the distributions shown in Table 9.6 suggest: Age produced a spurious association between the independent and dependent variables.

Table 9.6. The relationship between education and number of children, by age of mother (hypothetical data)

Number of children	Age 15–19 Years of education			Age 20–24 Years of education			Age 25–29 Years of education		
	<12	12	>12	<12	12	>12	<12	12	>12
1 or more	88%	88%	88%	92%	92%	92%	95%	95%	95%
None	12	12	12	8	8	8	5	5	5
Total number	67	300	133	67	300	133	66	300	134
%	100	100	100	100	100	100	100	100	100

If the associations shown in Table 9.4 are maintained for some categories of a control variable but not others, we would conclude that a condition has been specified under which the independent and dependent variables are associated. This is the case in Table 9.7, where the control variable is age. The number of children increases as the level of education rises for women aged fifteen to nineteen but not for the older women. We conclude that the independent and dependent variables may be causally related among the younger but not the older women. This should lead to further analyses to determine if the association among younger women is produced spuriously by some other variable.

Table 9.7. The relationship between education and number of children, by age of mother (hypothetical data)

Number of children	Age 15–19 Years of education			Age 20–24 Years of education			Age 25–29 Years of education		
	<12	12	>12	<12	12	>12	<12	12	>12
1 or more	60%	85%	98%	95%	95%	95%	98%	98%	98%
None	40	15	2	5	5	5	2	2	2
Total number	67	300	133	67	300	133	66	300	134
%	100	100	100	100	100	100	100	100	100

What is the basis for drawing such conclusions when a third variable occurs in contingency table analysis? In controlling for a third variable, we are essentially removing the effects of that variable from the relationship between two other variables. In the above example, we want to know if there is an association between education and number of children when the influence of women's age has been neutralized. If such a relationship is found among women aged fifteen to nineteen, then it cannot be due to the greater formal education and number of children among the older women because they have been excluded from the subtable analysis. If an initial relationship between education and number of children disappears when the effects of age have been removed by studying the relationship among different age groups, then that original relationship was attributable to age.

Intervening variables

After age and other variables that might produce a spurious association have been ruled out by controlled study, and we have a strong inference that independent and dependent variables are causally related, there is still the possibility that another kind of variable could explain the relation by *intervening* between them. Income, for instance, might explain why education and number of children are causally related. Perhaps the more education that women acquire, the wealthier they become. If women with more income are less concerned about the economic costs of children than women with less income, then perhaps education determines the number of children through its influence on income. A third variable that varies *after* the independent variable but *before* the dependent variable and explains why these two variables are causally associated is called an *intervening variable.*

Intervening variables are identified in the same way as variables that produce spurious associations. Thus, in the above examples, income can be substituted for age. The relationship between education and whether women have one or more children might be analyzed within the following categories of annual income: (1)<$3,000, (2) $3,000–$5,999, (3) $6,000–$8,999, (4) $9,000 and more. If controlling for income in this way yields subtables which still show associations between education and number of children, we can conclude that education does not influence number of children through its impact on income. If the associations disappear in all subtables, then we conclude that income might explain why education is related to the number of children. If the original relationship remains in some subtables but not others, we have identified the subgroups for which the inference that the intervening variable explains a causal relationship between independent and dependent variables might be made.

Given identical rules of conclusion when looking for intervening variables and variables that might produce spurious associations, how do we know when we have found one and not the other? If there is evidence that the third variable varied before the dependent variable and after the independent variable, then the control variable is considered an intervening variable. That is, we reason that the independent variable (education) influenced the intervening variable (income), which in turn influenced the dependent variable (number of children). Since education would not determine a person's age, age could not be considered an intervening variable if we found that it explained an initial relationship between education and number of children.

An example from an actual study

Hypothetical data formed the tables presented above. The application of contingency table analysis will now be summarized by using real data from research on the relationship between smoking behavior during pregnancy and birth weight that was conducted by Russell, Taylor, and Law (1968). This group gathered information on smoking behavior during pregnancy from a panel of about 2,000 women and then related these variables to birth weight. Among other hypotheses, two that shaped the study were:

1. Women who smoke during pregnancy have babies with lower birth weight than women who do not smoke during pregnancy because smoking causes high blood pressure, which in turn reduces birth weight.

2. The relationship between smoking and birth weight is not due to selected social, demographic, and physical variables.

Although it was not explicitly stated in their report, the researchers appeared to view blood pressure as a variable that might intervene between smoking and birth weight. Therefore, they wanted to determine if it explained why smoking and birth weight are causally related. The social, demographic, and physical variables encompassed by the second hypothesis were viewed as variables that might produce a spurious association between smoking and birth weight.

Two comments must be made before we present the contingency tables from this study. First, in the hypothetical examples above, percentages were used; in the tables presented below, the dependent variable—birth weight—is summarized as a mean. Interpretation is the same whether means or percentages are used. Second, the following contingency tables look somewhat different from those presented above. There is no standard format for contingency tables, so that extra effort is required when examining tables prepared by others.

Table 9.8 shows the relationship between smoking behavior and mean birth weight when controlling for blood pressure. The table is read by comparing the values for the dependent variable (birth weight) across categories of the independent variable (smoking behavior) within categories of the control variable (blood pressure). Within each of the three blood pressure categories, smokers have babies with lower mean birth weight than nonsmokers. The conclusion is that blood pressure does not explain the relationship between prenatal smoking behavior and birth weight, and therefore the first hypothesis is rejected.

Table 9.9 shows the relationship between smoking behavior and birth weight within categories of selected social, demographic, and physical variables. The purpose of this analysis is to determine if any of these other variables produce the association between smoking during pregnancy and birth weight. The table again is read by comparing the values of the dependent variables across categories of the independent variable within categories of the

Table 9.8. Fetal weights (oz.) for nonsmokers and smokers by maternal blood pressure levels

	Means	
	Foetal weight (oz.)	
Blood pressure	Nonsmokers	Smokers
<140/90	117.2	107.2
Occasionally or usually 140/90	114.2	108.9
≥150/100	99.3	90.8

Adapted from : C. Scott Russell, R. Taylor, and C. E. Law (1968) "Smoking in Pregnancy, Maternal Blood Pressure, Pregnancy Outcome, Baby Weight and Growth, and Other Related Factors." *British Journal of Preventive and Social Medicine* 22:119–26.

control variable. Since smokers had babies with lower mean birth weight than nonsmokers within the categories of each control variable, it is concluded that none of these variables explain the relationship between smoking behavior and birth weight. These results strengthen the inference that smoking and birth weight are causally related because the association is not attributable to such factors as parents' social class, maternal age, parity, attitude to pregnancy, and work experience. However, the association could be spuriously produced by variables not considered in this study, and therefore causality still is only inferred.

Other considerations

Tests of statistical significance are often used to analyze contingency tables. These tests have been ignored in this chapter since they will be the subject of the next one.

Contingency table analyses sometimes begin by exploring the possibility of associations between the control and independent variables and the control and dependent variables. A control variable must be associated with both the independent and dependent variables in order to account for an association between them. When control variables are associated with both independent and dependent variables, and in compatible directions, the relationships should then be viewed within categories of the con-

Table 9.9. Mean Fetal Weights (oz.)

Possible associated factors		Nonsmokers	Smokers	Total
Consort's social class	½	119.8	111.9	118.1
	3	116.4	106.8	113.4
	⁴⁄₅	114.2	106.0	111.1
Maternal age (yrs)	15–	115.9	108.7	113.8
	25–	116.8	105.0	113.4
	35–	116.1	108.3	112.9
Parity	1	115.1	106.6	112.9
	2/3/4	117.4	107.9	114.3
	≧5	116.0	105.1	111.4
Father's social class	½	118.5	111.1	116.7
	3	116.9	106.6	113.8
	⁴⁄₅	115.1	107.5	112.5
Possession of general certificate of education	Yes	119.2	110.5	117.5
	No	115.9	106.6	112.8
Consort's age (yrs)	15–	113.4	110.1	112.4
	25–	117.8	106.0	114.4
	35–	115.9	106.7	112.3
Maternal height	≧5′ 5″	120.4	114.4	118.4
	5′ 1″–5′ 4″	116.6	107.5	113.6
	Under 5′ 1″	113.1	103.4	109.9
Attitude to pregnancy	Wanted	116.4	107.3	113.6
	Doubtful	116.7	107.2	113.5
	Not wanted	115.5	104.5	111.4
1st trimester	None	117.2	106.9	113.8
	Part-time	116.5	105.2	113.0
	Full-time	115.2	107.4	112.8
2nd trimester	None	116.7	107.0	113.5
Work	Part-time	116.2	108.3	113.8
	Full-time	115.7	106.6	113.0
3rd trimester	None	116.6	107.2	113.6
	Part-time	117.8	115.4	117.4
	Full-time	118.8	111.6*	116.7

*Only 5 cases.
Adapted from: C. Scott Russell, R. Taylor, and C. E. Law (1968) "Smoking in Pregnancy, Maternal Blood Pressure, Pregnancy Outcome, Baby Weight and Growth, and Other Related Factors." *British Journal of Preventive and Social Medicine* 22: 119–26.

trol variables using the procedures and rules of interpretation described above.

Analyses do not necessarily end when no association is found between the independent and dependent variables. A third variable might be obscuring an important association. Indeed, a relationship that is causal in nature might be hidden by a third variable. For example, we might initially find that there is no relationship between education and number of children. However, there could be an association among urban but not rural women that is obscured if most of the study cases are from rural areas. Thus, we would need to control for place of residence, just as we did for age, to determine if there is an association within categories of that variable.

The examples that have been used to illustrate contingency table analysis in this chapter represent studies with nonintervention designs. However, the principles are directly applicable to intervention studies and to descriptive research that examines noncausal associations. In studies with intervention designs, the categories for the independent variables are formed through the design itself. For example, some receive a program while others do not, or varying types or amounts of programs are received, and these groups are then compared with respect to the dependent variable. In descriptive studies, the methods for examining associations between variables are the same except that we would not attempt to infer causality from the resulting tables.

Limitations of contingency table analysis

Although the above examples have been restricted to three variables—examining the relationship between the independent and dependent variables when controlling for a third variable—contingency table analyses are often used when more than three variables are considered simultaneously. The rules for constructing and interpreting such tables are the same as those described above. However, when the sample size is not extremely large, and variables are added, some cells of the tables may contain very few cases and others may even be empty. This precludes meaningful comparisons since we cannot determine if associations exist. Some variables are distributed so that this can occur for the two- or three-variable contingency table, as when cases in categories of a variable are rare in the population. One way to handle the problem is to gather data from a very large number of cases, but this may be too costly. Another approach is to collapse categories. For example, if cross-classification of a variable with education yields too few cases in the group with more than 12 years of education, we could combine these cases with the group having 12 years of education. This, of course, eliminates the higher education group from comparison, which might obscure important relationships. Moreover, categories cannot be collapsed indefinitely. Another approach is to use very few variables in the analysis, but this is not very satisfactory with the typical research problem, in which many different variables might be important. One major limitation of contingency table analysis is that either a very large number of cases is required or fewer variables than might be desired are included in the analysis.

Another problem of contingency table analysis is that it usually requires grouping cases in broad categories; this can result in a loss of meaningful information. For example, when using three educational categories (under 12, 12, and over 12) rather than the entire continuum of years of education to analyze the influence of this variable, persons with eleven years of education are not distinguished from those with none at all. Or when the control variable is age, there may be important differences within the age groups—for example, among women aged fifteen to nineteen.

With some variables we lack meaningful criteria for determining the cutoff points for the categories. It is relatively easy to establish categories for a variable such as education in the United States. The years of education used in the foregoing examples correspond roughly to "not a high school graduate," "high school graduate," and "education beyond high school," and these are meaningful categories in social, psychological, and economic terms. However, variables such as psychological stress, drug abuse, and maternal attachment are less easy to categorize. If attachment is measured on a 100-point scale, and we arbitrarily create three groups for contingency tables analysis—those with scores less than 33, 33 to 66, and over 66—this may not provide an accurate classification of people as being low, medium, and high in attachment. That is why researchers using contingency tables sometimes set different cutoff points in categorizing their data: to see if the formation of different categories produces varying results.

Another problem, not limited to contingency table analysis, is that relationships do not always come out as clear as they do in our examples. The relationships may be nonlinear rather than linear. For example, means for dependent variables might increase from 1.0 to 4.0 and then decline to 1.5 across categories of the independent variable rather than increase in a neat linear pattern from 1.0 to 1.5 to 4.0. The former distribution is often more difficult to interpret than the latter.

Despite these problems, contingency table analysis is one of the most valuable and frequently used approaches in biomedical and social science research.

Other methods of controlling for spurious associations

Several other methods have been described which control for variables that might produce spurious associations. They are mentioned again here so that their major strengths and weaknesses can be considered along with those of contingency table analysis.

The random allocation of cases to experimental and control groups in order to form categories of independent variables in intervention studies is nearly always the method preferred for reducing the chance of spurious associations. When random allocation cannot be employed, contingency tables are often used for analyzing the data.

Variables that might produce spurious associations can also be controlled by eliminating categories of the control variables. In studying the relationship between smoking behavior and birth weight, for example, education can be controlled by including only those with 12 years of education. Under that condition, years of education cannot produce an association between smoking and birth weight. The method of elimination is generally used when there are relatively few cases for some categories of the control variable in the population, and limited funds preclude gathering data from enough of these cases to allow contingency table analysis. The main disadvantage of control through elimination is that it usually restricts the generalization of findings to those represented by the single category of the control variable. Findings from a study of smoking and birth weight in women with 12 years of education might not apply to women who are college graduates or who did not finish high school. This problem is compounded when we are concerned with many variables that might be producing spurious associations, as is usually the case. Controlling for these variables by omitting many of their categories may yield a very narrow group for study and generalization.

Another way to control for variables which might be producing spurious associations is to match cases on the control variables either before or after collecting the data. For each smoker who has 12 years of education, we select a nonsmoker with 12 years of education; for each smoker who has 4 years of education, we select a nonsmoker with 4 years of education; and so forth. This yields groups of smokers and nonsmokers with similar education so that if there is an association between smoking and birth weight, it cannot be attributed to differences in years of education. This method is sometimes used to reduce the expense of research below that of studies using contingency table analysis when cases representing some categories of control variables are rare relative to other categories. One limitation of the case-matching method is that we are seldom satisfied with controlling for only one variable, and when other variables are added, we soon find that there is an insufficient number of cases to make all the matches needed.

In addition to these methods of control, several statistical tests are especially appropriate for identifying associations, spurious relationships, and intervening variables. These methods are discussed in the next chapter.

Reference

Russell, C. Scott; Taylor, R.; and Law, C.E. (1968) "Smoking in Pregnancy, Maternal Blood Pressure, Pregnancy Outcome, Baby Weight and Growth, and Other Related Factors." *British Journal of Preventive and Social Medicine* 22:119–26.

10
Statistical Significance and Strength

Tests of statistical significance are analysis techniques commonly used to help determine whether to accept or reject a hypothesis. Some of the tests gauge the strength of relationship between variables, some are specifically designed for analyses involving more than two variables, and others are especially appropriate for use in descriptive research. The purpose of this chapter is not to describe the individual tests but to present fundamental features of statistical significance and strength that govern their use.

Levels of significance

For the sake of clarity, and to be most consistent with the logic that underlies tests of statistical significance, the term *null hypothesis* must be introduced first. A null hypothesis usually specifies that there will be no association between variables. One example is the hypothesis that the babies of smokers and non-smokers will weigh the same at birth.

Even when research has been conducted carefully, the wrong decision can be made about a null hypothesis. Earlier chapters addressed some of the reasons for such mistakes. For instance, the research design may be inappropriate for testing the hypothesis or measurement may be invalid and insufficiently precise. Another reason derives from the fact that a hypothesis usually pertains to a population but the data used to test the hypothesis are usually obtained from a sample of the population. The inherent problem in this approach was discussed in Chapter 7: Distributions in a sample will usually not be identical to the distributions in the population. If one were very unlucky in selecting a sample, the sample cases might be quite different from most other cases in the population with respect to the variables of interest. Therefore, one might accept a null hypothesis through use of sample data when a relationship between the variables exists in the population, or one might reject a null hypothesis on the basis of sample data when there is no association between the variables in the population. Suppose data had been collected from a probability sample to test the hypothesis that there is no relationship between smoking and birth weight. The average weight of the babies of smokers was 108 ounces, and the average weight of the babies of nonsmokers was 114 ounces. If the null hypothesis is rejected—a decision that appears to be compatible with findings from the sample—what are the chances that the sample is so different from most other samples of the population that an incorrect decision is made about the relationship between smoking and birth weight in the population?

Fortunately, the chances that distributions in a probability sample approximate distributions for the population can be estimated without knowing the actual distributions in the population, a principle discussed in Chapter 7. Statistical tests permit explicit statements about the probability that the wrong conclusion will be made about the population sampled. Before calculating a test of statistical significance, let's say that in rejecting the null hypothesis we would be willing to accept a risk of as much as a 5 in 100 that there is no association between smoking and birth weight in the population. Since the actual distributions for the population are unknown, it is necessary to accept some chance of being wrong. The acceptable probability of being wrong about the population when a null hypothesis is rejected is called the *level of significance.* It is often symbolized as α. Thus, we have chosen α = .05. Using data from the sample to calculate a test of statistical significance, one might learn that the chances are 3 in 100 that there is no relationship between smoking and birth weight in the population. This value derived from the statistical test is often symbolized as *p*. Since *p* = .03 is less than α = .05, the null hypothesis would be rejected. The researcher would probably conclude from this that there is a statistically significant association between smoking and birth weight, and that the chances are quite good that a comparable relationship exists in the population from which the sample was drawn. Had *p* been greater than .05—say *p* = .10 or .20— then the null hypothesis would have been accepted. It would have been concluded that there was no statistically significant relationship between smoking and birth weight in the population even though, in the sample, the birth weights of babies of smokers and nonsmokers were different.

It is common practice for researchers to establish α at .05. Indeed, when reporting their studies, researchers frequently give only the statistical values for *p* that were generated and do not mention what level of significance was used for accepting and rejecting hypotheses. When this is done, it is usually assumed that α was set at .05. However, levels of significance other than .05 are used. To reduce the chances of rejecting a null hypothesis erroneously, α can be established at such levels as .01 or .001. These more stringent levels of significance may be used if rejection of the null hypothesis could lead to serious harm or large expenditures of money. In comparing the effects of a traditional social services program with a radically different program, for example, one would want to be quite certain that the new program is superior because it will be very expensive to initiate on a large scale. By setting α at less than .05, one would make it more difficult to reject the null hypothesis. On the other hand, α might be set at .10 if a research project is at the exploratory stage, when hypotheses are being tested for the purpose of deleting those independent variables which are not related to the dependent variable. At this point, one should not eliminate variables which are on the borderline of acceptable levels of statistical significance and might prove useful in subsequent phases of the study.

Two-variate tests and level of measurement

Many different tests of statistical significance are calculated by using sample information on two variables. These are called *two-variate tests*. There are many different two-variate tests to account for the many ways in which data differ. One major difference is with respect to the level of measurement of the variables; this is often the criterion for choosing the test that is used. The three levels of measurement most frequently encountered in community health and welfare research are *nominal, ordinal,* and *interval.*

At the nominal level of measurement, cases within categories of a variable are similar but the cases differ across categories. Also, unlike ordinal and interval levels of measurement, the categories cannot be ranked in a meaningful way. Examples of nominal level variables, and their categories, are:

Variable	*Categories*
Sex	Male and female
Region	North, South, East, and West
Clinic type	Fee for service and free
Religion	Protestant, Catholic, and Jewish

The ordinal level of measurement is similar to the nominal level except that for each variable the categories can be ranked meaningfully. That is, it can be reasoned that cases in one category are "greater than" or "higher than" or larger than" cases in other categories. Examples of ordinal level variables, and their categories, are:

Variable	Categories
Social class	Upper, middle, and lower
Attachment	Extremely attached, somewhat attached, not very attached, and unattached
Attitude toward clinic	Favorable and unfavorable
Level of education	Elementary, secondary, undergraduate college, and graduate school

It is meaningful to say that persons in the upper class rank higher than those in the middle class and that those in the middle class rank higher than those in the lower class. Similarly, persons who are extremely attached are more attached than those who are somewhat attached.

The interval level of measurement is the same as the ordinal level except for an additional property: The exact distances or "intervals" between categories are known. Examples of interval level variables, and their categories, are:

Variable	Categories
Smoking behavior	Number of cigarettes smoked
Birth weight	Ounces
Income	Dollars
Height	Inches

A baby weighing 114 ounces at birth weighs exactly 14 more ounces than a baby who weighs 100 ounces at birth, and this difference in ounces is equivalent to the interval between babies weighing 114 and 128 ounces at birth. It cannot be assumed that the intervals between upper, middle, and lower class are of equal distance. It makes little sense to say that the difference between lower and middle class is the same as the difference between middle and upper class, or that upper-class people have twice as much social class as middle-class people.

Table 10.1. Level of measurement and selected two-variate tests of statistical significance

1 Null hypothesis	2 Variable Independent	Dependent	3 Level of Measurement * Independent	Dependent	4 Selected tests of statistical significance †
1. There is no relationship between region and clinic type.	region	clinic type	nominal	nominal	chi square
2. There is no difference in the birth weight of boys and girls	sex	birth weight	nominal	interval	t-test (means) analysis of variance
3. There is no association between social class and attachment.	social class	attachment	ordinal	ordinal	Kendall tau Spearman's r_s gamma
4. Family income and birth weight are not related.	family income	birth weight	interval	interval	r (product-moment correlation)

* Assuming the variables were measured as described earlier in this chapter.
† These tests are discussed in detail in Blalock (1972).

To match a test with a particular set of data using the level of measurement criterion, the independent and dependent variables in the hypothesis are first identified, and then the level of measurement that most closely approximates each variable is determined. Four null hypotheses are listed in the first column of Table 10.1. The second column indicates the independent and dependent variables for each hypothesis. The variables are classified according to level of measurement in the third column. The fourth column lists selected tests of statistical significance that are especially appropriate for each level of measurement.

Many criteria in addition to level of measurement must be considered before choosing a particular test of statistical significance. They are beyond our scope here, but statistics texts and statisticians are useful resources. Moreover, we must recognize that a variable classified at one level of measurement in one study might be appropriately treated at another level in another study. Indeed, sometimes this occurs within the same study. For example, birth weight might be categorized by ounces for one analysis (interval level), or according to above normal, normal, and below normal birth weight (ordinal level) in another analysis. Also, the level of measurement criterion is an ideal, serving as a general rather than an absolute guide for choice among tests.

Statistical significance and contingency table analysis

When the relationship between two variables is being examined in a contingency table, a two-variate statistical test is often used to help determine if the hypothesis should be accepted or rejected. In a sample, the average birth weights of babies born to smokers and nonsmokers were 108 and 114 ounces respectively. We must determine if this is a statistically significant difference, and before doing this α is established at .05. An appropriate statistical test, according to Table 10.1, is the "t-test (means)": Smoking behavior is being considered at the nominal level (smokers versus nonsmokers), and birth weight was measured at the interval level (ounces). In addition to knowing the means, to calculate the t-test it is necessary to know for both smokers and nonsmokers the number of cases upon which the mean was based and the *variance*, which is a measure of the spread of cases around the mean. This information is entered in the formula for the t-test, which reveals that the value for t is equal to 4.96. With this value and known distributions prepared by statisticians, it is learned that $p = .03$. Thus, the chances are better than 5 in 100 that this association is approximated in most samples of the population. On this basis the null hypothesis is rejected, and it is concluded that there is a statistically significant relationship between smoking and birth weight.

Some of these tests are also used frequently in conjunction with contingency table analysis when more than two variables are of interest. If the hypothesis that there is no relationship between smoking and birth weight had been rejected, it would then be desirable to determine if the relationship was spurious as a result of such variables as maternal age and parity, or important to determine if blood pressure could explain why smoking influences birth weight. When contingency table analysis is used for these purposes, a statistical test of significance is calculated for the relationship between the independent and dependent variables within each category of the control variable, and then the rules of analysis presented here and in the preceding chapter are applied. As an example, Table 9.8 is repeated here as Table 10.2. After α was set at .05, a t-test was applied to the average birth weights of smokers and nonsmokers within each blood pressure category. The p's derived from t-tests for the two lower blood pressure levels were $<.05$, but for the highest blood pressure group the p was larger than .05. Thus, the null hypothesis for the two lower blood pressure groups is rejected, and it is accepted for the highest blood pressure group.

Some two-variate tests of statistical significance do not require portrayal of information in a contingency table format. A very popular test of this type is r (often called the *product-moment correlation coefficient* or *Pearson r*). As indicated in Table 10.1, r is especially appropriate for testing a null hypothesis concerning the association between two variables which are measured at the

Table 10.2. Mean fetal weights (oz.) for nonsmokers and smokers by maternal blood pressure levels

Blood pressure	Nonsmokers	Smokers	t	p
<140/90	117.2	107.2	8.2	<.05
140/90	114.2	108.9	2.0	<.05
>150/100	99.3	90.8	1.3	>.05

Adapted from: C. Scott Russell, R. Taylor, and C. E. Law (1968) "Smoking in Pregnancy, Maternal Blood Pressure, Pregnancy Outcome, Baby Weight and Growth, and Other Related Factors." *British Journal of Preventive and Social Medicine* 22: 119–126.

interval level. It might be hypothesized that there is no association between family income measured in dollars and birth weight measured in ounces. Before calculating r, α is set at .05. Information from the sample is entered in the appropriate formula and r is found to equal .36. The question now is whether this value of .36 for r is statistically significant. That is, if the null hypothesis is rejected on the basis of this value for r, are the chances good that there is an association between income and birth weight in the population? Viewing the r of .36 and known distributions prepared by statisticians, it is concluded that the chances are 2 in 100 that there is no relationship between the variables in the population. Given these odds the hypothesis is rejected, and it is concluded that the relationship between income and birth weight is statistically significant. The tests in Table 10.1 which involve ordinal measurement of both variables are more similar to r than the other two-variate tests with nominal level of measurement in the sense that means and percentages are not necessarily viewed in the contingency table format when they are used.

Multivariate tests

For the statistical tests discussed thus far, sample data from only two variables are involved in the actual calculation of a test. The data on smoking and birth weight were used in calculating the t-tests described above, and although blood pressure was included in Table 10.2, sample information on that variable was not entered into the formula for the test. Another group of tests is especially appropriate for analyses involving more than two variables which include sample information from more than two variables as part of the calculation. They are commonly called *multivariate tests*. These tests do not require portrayal of data in the contingency table format. Like two-variate tests, multivariate tests are used to gauge statistical significance in order to provide assistance in making decisions about null hypotheses. In addition, multivariate tests usually allow consideration of more data in relatively efficient and informative ways than two-variate tests.

Since many research problems involve many different variables, multivariate tests are very important analytical tools. For example, much research is conducted in an attempt to identify all variables which might have an influence upon a dependent variable. In such cases, it is usually necessary to determine which of the independent variables are significantly associated with the dependent variable, to attempt to control simultaneously for variables that might be producing spurious relationships, and to determine how much the independent variables when considered together influence the dependent variable. Kandel and her colleagues (1976) tested hypotheses about the relationships between sixteen social psychological variables and marijuana smoking behavior in a cross-sectional study of adolescents. They were interested in answering such questions as: (1) Are peer, parental, and other characteristics associated with marijuana smoking behavior? (2) Is peer behavior more important than parent behavior in influencing marijuana smoking behavior? (3) Are any of these relationships spurious? (4) How much is marijuana smoking behavior influenced by all sixteen independent variables combined? They applied a form of regression analysis—a multivariate test—which provided the information necessary to make decisions about all these questions. In the analysis, all the variables were being considered together and, as with two-variate tests, the statistical significance of associations was established.

Had Kandel and her collaborators chosen a contingency table analysis strategy with two-variate tests, they would have immediately encountered problems. First, because they were interested in identifying intervening variables, and variables that might have produced spurious associations, they would have had to generate a very large number of contingency tables within all combinations of categories of each control variable. They would have soon discovered cells in their contingency tables that contained no cases and many more cells with very few cases. That would have made it impossible to use most two-variate tests of statistical significance, and with some cells empty even through visual inspection there would have been no way to determine if associations existed. Secondly, they would have generated so many contingency tables that interpretation would have been difficult if not impossible. Thirdly, the combined influence of all independent variables on the dependent variable could not have been estimated with two-variate tests.

Multivariate tests are used in many other ways. Bauman and Udry (1972) hypothesized that there would be no relationship between how men felt about the control they had over their lives and how regularly they used contraceptives. The 350 men in their sample who responded to seven items designed to measure "powerlessness" were asked how regularly they used contraception and were questioned on other variables considered to be potentially important to the relationship between a sense of powerlessness and contraceptive behavior. A contingency table used in conjunction with a two-variate statistical test resulted in rejection of the null hypothesis. The next step was to analyze powerlessness and eight other variables which might have produced a spurious relationship between powerlessness and regularity of contraception. For one of the analyses, a multivariate test (a form of multiple regression) was applied to control simultaneously for the eight variables, and it was found that powerlessness and regularity of contraception were still associated ($\alpha = .05$). Thus, through the application of one multivariate test rather than a proliferation of contingency tables in conjunction with two-variate tests, it was possible to conclude that the relationship between powerlessness and regularity of contraception was not spurious as a result of the eight other variables.

As with two-variate tests of statistical significance, different

Table 10.3. Selected multivariate tests of statistical significance

1	2 Variable			3 Level of Measurement*			4 Selected tests of
Null hypothesis	Independent	Dependent	Control	Independent	Dependent	Control	statistical significance †
1. There is no relationship between income and birth weight when controlling for smoking behavior (number of cigarettes smoked) and height.	income	birth weight	smoking behavior height	interval	interval	interval	partial r multiple regression
2. There is a relationship between religion and smoking behavior after controlling for income.	religion	smoking behavior	income	nominal	interval	interval	analysis of covariance

* Assuming the variables were measured as described earlier in this chapter.
† These tests are discussed in detail in Blalock (1972).

multivariate tests are used with different forms of data, and the level of measurement of the variables is a major criterion for choosing among the tests. Three of the more commonly used multivariate tests, with illustrative null hypotheses and appropriate levels of measurement, are shown in Table 10.3.

Sample size and fraction

Studies are sometimes criticized when they use small samples, and on this basis alone it is concluded that reasonable decisions cannot be made about hypotheses. Whereas this criticism is sometimes justified, it can be tempered when tests of statistical significance have been used appropriately; for reasons related to our discussion of sample size and confidence intervals in Chapter 7, these tests take sample size into account. If a null hypothesis is rejected on the basis of appropriate application of a test of statistical significance, it can usually be concluded that the sample was not too small. If, on the other hand, the null hypothesis of no association is accepted through use of a test, then this might be because the sample was too small.

When all other things remain equal, the larger the sample size the greater the chance that a null hypothesis will be rejected. Table 10.4 illustrates this relationship between statistical significance and sample size. The hypothesis is that there is no association between smoking behavior and birth weight. In each hypothetical sample, the number of cases is split evenly between smokers and nonsmokers, and 10 percent of the smokers have low birth weight babies. The total sample sizes vary from 100 to 800. The far right column shows the percentages of low birth weight babies necessary among the nonsmokers in order to conclude that the hypothesis should be rejected at $\alpha = .05$. It can be seen from the table that as sample size increases, smaller differences between the percentages of smokers and nonsmokers with low birth weight babies are necessary to reject the null hypothesis. If 10 percent of a sample of 50 smokers have low birth weight babies, either less than 2 percent or more than 18 percent of the 50 nonsmokers must

Table 10.4. Percentages required to reject the null hypothesis at α = .05 for different sample sizes when the percentage for one category = 10

			Percentage with low birth weight babies	
Sample Size	Smokers	Nonsmokers	Smokers	Nonsmokers*
100	50	50	10	<2 or >18
200	100	100	10	<4 or >16
400	200	200	10	<6 or >14
800	400	400	10	<7 or >13

*Percentage required to reject null hypothesis at α = .05.

have low birth weight babies to reject the null hypothesis. If there had been 800 cases in the sample and 10 percent of the smokers had low birth weight babies, then less than 7 percent or more than 13 percent of the nonsmokers would have had to have low birth weight babies in order for the null hypothesis to be rejected at α = .05.

The chance of rejecting the null hypothesis through use of a test of statistical significance increases with sample size. This fact sometimes makes these tests inappropriate for use with very large samples. When statistical significance is used to test associations between two variables in samples of 100,000 cases, the chances are quite good that most null hypotheses involving any two variables would be rejected even when the link between variables is not meaningful. Thus, it can be misleading to use tests of statistical significance for accepting and rejecting null hypotheses when data are from very large samples.

Another reservation which relates to sample size is that a hypothesis cannot be tested with acceptable accuracy when the sample represents only a small fraction of the population. How can an inference about a population of 100,000 be made on the basis of a random sample of only 300, or .3 percent of the population? As we saw in Chapter 7, the number of cases in a sample is usually much more important than the sampling fraction for drawing reasonable inferences about a population. This principle extends to testing null hypotheses about populations when applying tests of statistical significance: Under most conditions for which a sample rather than an entire population would be studied, the sampling fraction makes a negligible contribution. Thus, the typical concern is whether there are enough cases to be able to reject a null hypotheses that should be rejected, and the sampling fraction is usually of less concern.

Strength of association

Statistical significance indicates whether an association in a sample is likely to exist in a population, but does not by itself reflect how strong an association is. The chance for rejecting a null hypothesis increases with sample size. This is one major reason that measures of strength of association are often necessary. A test applied to a very large sample might yield a $p = .01$, but that association might be weak. When comparing two associations in samples of different sizes, if we want to determine whether one relationship is stronger than the other (as is often the case), then the appropriate test for strength of association is necessary. The values yielded by the significance test might be reflecting the sample size more than the strength of the relationship.

Knowledge of the strength of a relationship is needed to answer many questions. Suppose there are statistically significant relationships between mother's education and number of children, and between father's education and number of children. That is, the null hypotheses about these relationships have been rejected at $\alpha = .05$. In both relationships, those with the least education have more children than those with higher education. After introducing controls for other variables considered to be relevant, we infer that the education of men and women has a causal influence on their number of children. If both statistically significant relationships are weak, this suggests that the independent variables have modest rather than important causal influences on the number of children. This has important practical implications if it is expected that the number of children will decrease as more people receive education: Given the weak associations, it is unlikely that an increase in the percentage of educated people would have a substantial effect on the birth rate. Moreover, finding these weak relationships might signal the need to conduct further studies in a search for variables that have stronger causal relationships with the number of children. If the relationship between mother's education and number of children was very strong, and the relationship between father's education and number of children was statistically significant but very weak, raising the level of education for men might not influence the number of children nearly as much as raising the educational level of women.

There are many different methods to assess strength of association. As is true for tests of statistical significance, one of the major criteria used in matching a particular test of strength to a particular set of data is that the test and levels of measurement are compatible. Table 10.5 lists hypotheses concerning the strength of association when two variables are involved, the levels of measurement for the variables, and selected two-variate measures of strength of association. All the multivariate tests listed in Table 10.3 yield values which, in addition to providing information necessary to determine whether relationships are statistically significant, help gauge the strength of relationships. The level of measurement of variables is only one of several criteria that govern the use of these techniques, and therefore the information we provide here is not sufficient for final decisions about which methods should be used. Nevertheless, this organization of tests can facilitate learning more about individual tests through sources other than this book.

Statistical and practical significance

Tests of statistical significance do not necessarily indicate practical significance. This is an important consideration for programs and policy that is frequently overlooked. Two examples will illustrate the problem.

A program administrator knows that there are 25,500 people in need of services who have never used the program. The admin-

Table 10.5. Selected two-variate tests of strength of association

Hypothesis	Variable Independent	Variable Dependent	Level of measurement* Independent	Level of measurement* Dependent	Two-variate test of strength †
1. The relationship between sex and region of residence is stronger than the relationship between hair color and region of residence.	sex hair color	region of residence	nominal	nominal	contingency coefficient phi lambda Cramer's V
2. The association between sex and smoking behavior is stronger than the association between region and smoking behavior.	sex region	smoking behavior	nominal	interval	intraclass correlation
3. On a scale from zero to 1.00, how strong is the relationship between income and birth weight?	income	birth weight	interval	interval	r^2 (square of product-moment correlation)

* Assuming the variables were measured as described earlier in this chapter.
† These tests are discussed in detail in Blalock (1972).

istrator's goal is to see that at least 15,000 of these people use the program. A study of a random sample of 500 of the 25,500 people reveals that 15 percent of the people contacted through extensive outreach activities use the program compared to only 5 percent of those who were not exposed to the outreach efforts. Through application of an appropriate test of statistical significance, the null hypothesis of no relationship between outreach and program use was rejected at $\alpha = .01$. This research was done so well as to convince everyone that extending the outreach to all 25,500 individuals would increase use of the program. But should outreach be implemented to achieve the goal of getting 15,000 members of the target population to use the program? From the research, it can be estimated that 2,500 of the 25,000 people would use the program as a result of the outreach effort (15 − 5 percent of 25,000 = 2,500). This is a long way from the goal of 15,000. Although the relationship between outreach and program use is statistically significant, it does not appear to be practically significant in view of the administrator's goal and the projected impact of outreach.

The second example places statistical and practical significance in a much different context. A study finds that there is a statistically significant relationship at $\alpha = .05$ between a measure of mother and infant characteristics (this measure includes such items as birth weight, gestation, age of mother, mother's education, and parity of mother) and the manifestation of developmental disabilities between birth and five years of age. It is decided to use the measure of infant characteristics for identifying which infants should be given special services between birth and five years of age so that their developmental disabilities can be prevented or the consequences minimized. One reason this decision may not be as fruitful as hoped is inherent in the statistical test: Although there is a statistically significant relationship between the measure of mother and infant characteristics at birth and subsequent developmental disabilities, this association might be weak. If so, many children in need of help would not be selected by the measure to receive services, while many who did not need the services would be selected. In this situation the measure of mother and infant characteristics is not likely to help prevent or minimize developmental disabilities for many children even if the services provided are extremely effective. This example has analogies in many health and welfare screening programs which identify high-risk cases for special treatment. Measures used for these purposes should be closely examined to see how strongly they correlate with the outcomes of interest in addition to determining whether the relationships are statistically significant.

Statistical significance in descriptive research

Thus far, statistical significance has been considered in terms of testing null hypotheses that involve two or more variables. Statistical significance is also used when considering one variable at a time, as is appropriate in many descriptive studies. Indeed, statistical tests were used in Chapter 7 to illustrate the relationship between sample size and confidence intervals for a percentage based on information from one variable. The study of trends in polio immunization among American children outlined in Chapter 6 reported confidence intervals at various levels of significance for the percentages of immunized persons. If we had to estimate the cost of immunizing 90 percent of the population, then a reasonable estimate of the percentage not immunized would be necessary. This can be derived by applying statistical significance to data from a sample of the population.

Table 10.6 illustrates how statistical significance was applied in another descriptive study. These data are from a random sample of unmarried university students who completed questionnaires in 1968. The nonvirgins in the sample were asked to indicate the method of contraception they usually used. Although 7 percent of the women said that they generally used the birth control pill, given the fact that this was based on only 43 women it was assumed that the value for the population could differ substantially from 7 percent. The percentage in the population was of particular interest because that was the group to be learned about through study of the sample. Thus, α was set at .05 and a test of statistical significance then calculated (in this case a z test). From

Table 10.6. Type of contraceptive generally used by sex

Contraceptive	No. (Men)	% (Men)	No. (Women)	% (Women)
Nothing	6	11.1 ± 8.5	0	0
Condom	28	51.8 ± 13.6	20	46.5 ± 15.4
Withdrawal	13	24.1 ± 11.7	12	27.9 ± 13.8
Diaphragm	0	0	0	0
Foam-jelly	1	1.8 ± 3.5	3	7.0 ± 7.8
Pill	4	7.4 ± 7.2	3	7.0 ± 7.8
Rhythm	2	3.7 ± 5.1	5	11.6 ± 9.7
IUD	0	0	0	0
Douche	0	0	0	0
Total	54	100.0	43	100.0

From: Karl E. Bauman (1970) Selected aspects of the contraceptive practices of unmarried university students. *American Journal of Obstetrics and Gynecology* 108: 203–209.

this it was learned that the chances were 95 in 100 that the percentage in the population who generally used the pill could be as high as 14.8 (7.0 ± 7.8) percent.

A variety of statistical tests described in Blalock (1972) and Dunn (1977) are used to make estimates such as these in descriptive research.

Tests of statistical significance and probability samples

Tests of statistical significance are based upon the known features of probability samples. Therefore, these tests are most appropriately applied to data from probability samples. However, since a perfect probability sample is rare, when tests of statistical significance are applied this ideal is seldom achieved. There are many reasons why perfect probability samples are not obtained. For example, the population total from which the sample was drawn may be incomplete or some cases selected for the sample may not enter the study. The more nearly the sample approximates a probability sample, however, the more confidence we have in decisions that are made using tests of statistical significance. If it can be assumed that a listing of the population is quite accurate, and that 80 percent of the cases selected for the sample are included in analyses, our confidence is high. If, on the other hand, a sample is drawn from a grossly inaccurate listing of the population, or the list is accurate but only 20 percent of the cases chosen for the sample provide the necessary data, then there is less confidence in decisions about hypotheses based on tests of statistical significance.

Other considerations

The principles discussed in this chapter are equally applicable when units other than people are used. For example, tests of statistical significance are used in testing null hypotheses when cities, states, and clinics are the units of analysis.

These principles are applicable to intervention as well as non-intervention designs, although most of the examples in this chapter are of the latter type. An intervention design could be used, for example, to test the null hypothesis that reduction in caseload is not related to a change in family functioning. The mean level of family functioning among families which received workers with different caseloads would be compared, and to determine if the difference in means is attributable to the difference in the workers' caseloads, an appropriate two-variate test of statistical significance would be applied. The strength of any relationship found could be determined with additional tests, and multivariate tests could be used if variables other than caseload and family functioning were added to the analysis.

Results that reveal statistically significant relationships are sometimes used as evidence of causality. Alone, however, they do not provide all the evidence necessary to make a causal inference. They do help determine the probability that a relationship which exists among variables in a sample also exists in the population. They are also valuable aids in analyzing whether associations are spurious, in identifying intervening variables, and in assessing the strength of relationships.

Statistics deal with probabilities rather than certainties. In making decisions about relationships among variables, the probabilities that our decisions are incorrect can be specified, but this can never be definite.

Blalock (1972) and Dunn (1977) are recommended for their discussions of tests of statistical significance and strength.

References

Bauman, Karl E. (1970) "Selected Aspects of Contraceptive Practices of Unmarried University Students." *American Journal of Obstetrics and Gynecology* 108:203–09.

———and Udry, J. Richard (1972) "Powerlessness and Regularity of Contraception in an Urban Negro Male Sample: A Research Note." *Journal of Marriage and the Family* 34:112–14.

Blalock, Hubert M. (1972) *Social Statistics.* New York: McGraw-Hill.

Dunn, Olive Jean (1977) *Basic Statistics: A Primer for the Biomedical Sciences.* New York: John Wiley and Sons.

Kandel, Denise B.; Treiman, Donald; Faust, Richard; and Single, Eric (1976) Adolescent Involvement in Legal and Illegal Drug Use: A Multiple Classification Analysis." *Social Forces* 55:438–58.

Russell, C. Scott; Taylor, R. and Law, C.E. (1968) "Smoking in Pregnancy, Maternal Blood Pressure, Pregnancy Outcome, Baby Weight and Growth, and Other Related Factors." *British Journal of Preventive and Social Medicine* 22:119–26.

Epilogue

Once again, it must be emphasized that the purpose of this book has been to provide an *introduction* to methods used in community health and welfare research. None of the methods was discussed in thorough detail, and some techniques that might have been addressed were not mentioned. This is compatible with the needs of most workers in community health and welfare, and I hope that readers who wish to go beyond this introduction will find the references useful.

The division of this book by chapters could leave the impression that the methods presented are less closely related than they really are. Their independence may have been most apparent in the last chapter, where at least some of the methods dealt with in each preceding chapter were drawn into the discussion of statistical significance and strength. Had any other chapter been the final one, then it too would have appeared more dependent on all earlier chapters.

Any introduction to a complex subject can leave the impression that things are more orderly than they actually are. If research did respond strictly to a set of rules, then the lives of researchers and others would be much simpler. However, it is rarely neat and tidy because innumerable factors influence the conduct of research. Nonetheless, studies conducted within a reasonable approximation of the ideal are essential in contributing to decisions about the health and welfare of communities. They do not provide definitive answers to our questions, but they are usually better guides to action than common sense, intuition, tradition, and authority.

Index

accidental sampling, 74
Alan Guttmacher Institute, The, 64
Albert, Joel J., 4
(alpha), 121
association
  contingency table analysis of,
    103–17
  in cross-sectional design, 52–55
  levels of significance for, 119–22
  in nonintervention designs, 60–62
  in one group-after only design,
    26–27
  in one group-before after design,
    30–35
  in panel design, 57–59
  sample size for tests of, 131–33
  strength of, 133–34
  tests of, 125–31
  in trend design, 55–56
  in two group-after only design,
    27–30
  in two group-before after design,
    36–39
attrition, 29–30, 35
  in panel design, 59
  in sampling, 76–77

Bauman, Karl E., 4, 24, 129
Becker, M.H., 11, 13, 14
bias, sources of. *See also* spuriousness
  attrition, 76–77
  sample size, 77–79
  selection, 75–76
Blalock, Hubert M., Jr., 16, 20, 138,
  140

Campbell, Donald T., 48
causality, 16–22. *See also*
  spuriousness
  absent in descriptive research, 64–67
  in contingency table analysis,
    106–14
  in cross-sectional design, 52–54
  in one group-after only design,
    26–27
  in one group-before after design,
    30–31
  in panel design, 57–58
  random allocation and, 40–43
  statistical significance and, 139
  in trend design, 55–56

causality (continued)
　in two group-after only design,
　　28–29
　in two group-before after design, 36
Center for Disease Control, U.S., 65
cluster samples, 72, 73
Cochran, William G., 69
confidence intervals, 77–79
construct validity, 96–97
contingency table analysis, 103–17
　multivariate tests and, 128–29
　statistical significance and, 125–27
control groups, random allocation to,
　40–42, 116
control variables, in contingency
　table analysis, 107–17
Cook, Stuart W., 101
costs of research, 68
criterion measures, 94–96
criterion-related validity, 94–96
Cronbach, Lee J., 101–2
cross-sectional design, 51–55

data
　collected without hypotheses, 9–10
　collection methods for, 100–101
　levels of measurement of, 122–25
dependent variables, 18–22
　additional, 47
　in contingency table analysis, 103,
　　105–9, 111–14
　in cross-sectional design, 52–54
　in four group-two before and four
　　after design, with random
　　allocation, 46
　in intervention designs, 23, 24
　in multivariate tests, 128–29
　in nonintervention designs, 60, 61
　in one group-after only design,
　　26–27
　in one group-before after design,
　　30–35
　in outcome evaluation, 48
　in panel design, 57–58
　random allocation and, 40–43
　in trend design, 55–56
　in two group-after only design,
　　27–30, 43
　in two group-before after design,
　　36–39, 44
descriptive research, 63–67

statistical significance in, 137–38
Diamond, Margaret, 50, 51
differential attrition, 29–30, 35
differential selection, 29
Dunn, Olive Jean, 138, 140

equal-appearing interval scales, 99
equivalence, 91–92
error, measurement, 85–88
　in choice of data collection method,
　　101
evaluation, 48–49
experimental groups, random
　allocation to, 40–42, 116

face validity, 92–93
fineness of measures, 100
four group-two before and four after
　design, with random allocation,
　45–46
fraction, sampling, 80, 132–33
Frazier, Todd M., 50

gambling analogy, 70
generalization
　cautions on, 44–45
　controlling for variables limiting
　　scope of, 117
　populations appropriate for, 68

Haar, Esther, 64
Haeri, A.D., 64
Halitsky, Victor, 64
health belief theory, 11–13
Higgins, Ian T., 55
history
　random allocation to control for,
　　41–42
　as source of spuriousness, 32–33, 45
hypotheses, 7–11
　construct validity testing of, 96–97
　contingency table analysis of, 103,
　　110–12
　levels of measurement for, 125

measurement and, 83–84
in nonintervention designs, 50–51
null, 119–21
populations implied by, 80–81
sample size for tests of, 131–33
theories and, 13–15

independent variables, 17–22
additional, 46–47
in contingency table analysis,
103–9, 111–14
in cross-sectional design, 52–54
in intervention designs, 23, 24
in multivariate tests, 128–29
in nonintervention designs, 50, 51,
61
in one group-after only design,
26–27
in one group-before after design,
30–35
in panel design, 57–58
random allocation and, 40–43
in trend design, 55–56
in two group-after only design,
27–30, 43
in two group-before after design,
36–39, 44
index measures, 94–97
inference
causal, in descriptive research,
66–67
causal, statistical significance and,
139
causality in, 18–20
instrumentation
fineness of measures and, 100
random allocation to control for, 42
as source of spuriousness, 34
internal consistency, 91–92
interobserver reliability, 92
interval data, 122, 123
r correlations for, 126–27
intervening variables, 22
in contingency table analysis,
106–12
intervention designs, 23–49
contingency table analysis in, 114
statistical significance in, 139
interviewing, measurement error in,
87

Kandel, Denise B., 50–52, 128
Kerlinger, Fred N., 15
Kish, Leslie, 69

Lastrucci, Carlo L., 15
Law, C.E., 110
levels of measurement, 122–25
multivariate tests for, 131
strength of tests and, 134
levels of significance, 119–22
Lundberg, George A., 84

Maiman, L.A., 11, 13, 14
matching, 39–40
in contingency table analysis, 117
in nonintervention designs, 60
maturation
random allocation to control for, 42
as source of spuriousness, 33–34
measurement, 83–102. See also levels
of measurement
measures, fineness of, 100
Mechanic, David, 50, 51
multiple-item scales, 97–99
multiple regression, 129
multivariate tests, 127–31
strength of, 134

Naldrett, Janet, 64
nominal data, 122
tests of significance for, 127
nonintervention designs, 50–62
contingency table analysis in, 114
nonprobability sampling, 73–75
null hypotheses, 119–21
sample size and rejection of, 131–33

one group-after only design, 25–27
one group-before after design, 30–35
ordinal data, 122–23
tests of significance for, 127
outcome evaluation, 48–49

p, 121
panel design, 56–59
parallel forms procedure, 90–91
Pearson *r*, 126–27
percentages, in contingency table analysis, 104–5, 111
populations, 68
  implied in hypotheses, 80–81
  sample size and fraction of, 131–33
  sampling of, 69–75
  significance levels and sampling of, 120
  tests of statistical significance and, 138–39
practical significance, 134–37
probability
  levels of significance and, 120–21
  nonprobability sampling and, 73–74
  in random allocation, 43
  in sampling, 69–73, 76
  tests of statistical significance and, 138–39
product-moment correlation coefficient (*r*), 126–27
propositions, hypotheses distinguished from, 8
purposive samples, 74, 75

quota samples, 74–75

r (product-moment correlation coefficient; Pearson *r*), 126–27
random allocation, 40–43
  in contingency table analysis, 116
random selection, 69, 72
regression analysis, 128
regression toward the mean, 34–35
  random allocation to control for, 42
reliability, 88–92, 97
  multiple-item scales for, 98
repeated measures, 34–35
research
  descriptive, 63–67
  hypotheses in, 7–10
  intervention designs in, 23–49
  nonintervention designs in, 50–62
  sampling for, 68–81

setting levels of significance for, 121–22
  theories in, 13–15
  value of, 4–5
Rosenstock, I.W., 11, 13, 14
Russell, C. Scott, 110

samples and sampling, 68–81. *See also* size of samples
  null hypothesis and, 120
  tests of statistical significance and, 138–39
sample selection
  bias in, 75–76
  matching in, 39–40
  in nonintervention designs, 60
  random allocation for, 40–43
  as source of spuriousness, 29
sampling fraction, 80, 132–33
scales
  levels of measurement for, 122–25
  multiple-item, 97–99
selection. *See* sample selection
self-selection, 29, 41
Selltiz, Claire, 101
significance, statistical, 119–40
  based on probability, 74
  in contingency table analysis, 112
simple random samples, 72
size of samples, 77–79
  in contingency table analysis, 114–15
  statistical significance and, 131–33
South, Joanna, 64
split-half technique, 91
spuriousness, 19
  in contingency table analysis, 106–10, 112, 116–17
  in cross-sectional design, 54–55
  in nonintervention designs, 60–61
  in panel design, 58–59
  random allocation to control for, 41–43
  sources of, 29–30, 32–35, 37–39. *See also* bias, sources of
  in trend design, 56
stability, 88–91
Stanley, Julian C., 48
statistical significance, 119–40

based on probability, 74
in contingency table analysis, 112
stratified random samples, 72–73
strength, statistical, 133–34
Stricker, George, 64
Stuart, Alan, 69
Suchmann, Edward A., 49
summated scales, 98
Summers, Gene F., 92, 102

Tagliacozzo, Daisy M., 4
Taylor, R., 110
Tessler, Richard, 50, 51, 56–57, 59
testing
  random allocation to control for, 42
  sample size for, 131–33
  as source of spuriousness, 34, 35, 46
  stability in, 89–91
  statistical significance for, 125–31
theories, 11–14
  construct validity testing of, 96–97
trend design, 55–56
t-tests, 125–26
two group-after only design, 27–30
  with random allocation, 43–44
two group-before after design, 35–39
  with random allocation, 44–45
two variate tests, 122–25
  strength of, 134

Udry, J. Richard, 129

validity, 88, 92–97
value judgments, 8
variables. See also dependent
    variables; independent variables
  additional, 21, 46–47
  additional, in nonintervention
    designs, 54–56, 59, 61
  contingency table analysis of,
    103–17
  in descriptive research, 64–65
  independent and dependent, 17–18
  inferring causality between, 18–20
  intervening, 22
  in intervention designs, 23, 24
  levels of significance for, 121–22
  matching by, 39–40
  measurement of, 83–88
  multivariate tests of, 127–31
  probability sampling and, 71–73
  random selection and, 69
  two-variate tests of, 122–25
variance, 126
Verbrugge, Lois M., 50

Wallace, David, 4, 23
Weiss, Carol H., 49
Wrightsman, Lawrence S., 101

Yerushalmy, J., 50